Fishers of Men

The Jesuit Mission at Mackinac
1670-1765

Brother James Boynton, S.J.

Introduction by
Phil Porter

Ste. Anne's Church,
Mackinac Island, Michigan
1996

To my Uncle and Brother

William Goudreau, S.J.

A Mackinac Jesuit in Patna, India

Imprimi Potest: Reverend Keith Esenther, S.J.
                      Acting Provincial, Detroit Province of the
                      Society of Jesus
                      February 15, 1996

Imprimatur: Most Reverend James H. Garland
                      Bishop of Marquette
                      February 27, 1996

TABLE OF CONTENTS

Foreword

I recall my first visit to Mackinac Island, standing on the ramparts of the Old Fort in 1948, looking down on the statue of Father Marquette thinking: "I'd like to be like him." Nearly half a century later I now have the great honor to be his successor as pastor of Ste. Anne's. So the past continues to call us to the present and beyond. So too for three hundred years Ste. Anne's has been a hand pointing the way to God, as it can with great clarity on an island where everyone knows "we're all in the same boat." To every Catholic, Protestant, Jew and Agnostic that Ste. Anne's serves she can also proclaim: "there is the Kingdom of God – within you." That is the Magic of Mackinac, the gospel of Christ and the Mission of the Church. As Ste. Anne's begins her Fourth Century we are pleased to offer Brother James Boynton's history as an adornment to that ancient pointing hand and as an enticement to make the journey that so many great men and women have made with her over the centuries.

May the past remain as prologue to the future. May each of us find and enter the Kingdom of God.

Father James M. Williams
Pastor, Ste. Anne's

Preface

By its constitution the Society of Jesus is a missionary society. The order has carried on the work of evangelization, which is proclaim Jesus as Lord and Savior, from its beginning. The conversion of the unbeliever and the salvation of souls moved St. Ignatius and his followers to travel literally to the ends of the earth. No other work save education has occupied more members of the Society.

My research revealed that in the seventeenth and eighteenth centuries 3500 Jesuits labored in North America, 329 of them in French territories. These included the Great Lakes region. By the time of the suppression in 1773, there were 122 Jesuits supervising 100 mission stations and serving 122,000 Native Americans.

FISHERS OF MEN completes a chapter of the Jesuit missions at Mackinac. Brother Boynton's work comes as a welcome compilation of the historical facts of the missionary labors of the Jesuit Fathers and Brothers, from Claude Dablon and Jacques Marquette to Joseph Lawless in our own day. This heritage of planters of the faith is a wellspring of inspiration and encouragement to all of us today who seek to undertake a new evangelization of the Americas as urged by our Holy Father, Pope John Paul II. Brother Boynton's work should help all of us of the Church of Marquette to prepare for the jubilee of Christ's 2000th birthday with enthusiastic zeal to continue the proclamation of the Good News into the Third Millennium of Christianity.

+James H. Garland
Bishop of Marquette

Introduction

Mackinac has a long, rich and fascinating history. This strategic cross-roads of the upper Great Lakes has been home to Native Americans, European fur traders, soldiers of three nations, commercial fishermen and summer vacationers. Mackinac's importance has ebbed and flowed over time. It has been a bustling, international port and an obscure, nearly deserted and very lonely northern Michigan outpost. As nations have come and gone, soldiers marched in and out, industries flourished and failed, there has been one constant since the 1670's – the presence of Roman Catholicism.

Roman Catholicism came to the Straits of Mackinac through the self-sacrificing efforts of Jesuit Missionaries. The early history of the entire Great Lakes region echoes with the names of Jesuit priests and brothers who traveled side-by-side, and sometimes ahead of, the first explorers and traders. With an unrelenting zeal to take the word of God to all people, men such as Jean de Brebeuf, Isaac Jogues, Charles Raymbault, Claude Allouez, Gabriel Druilletes, Rene Goupil and Claude Dablon journeyed to the far reaches of the Great Lakes and to the Straits of Mackinac in 1670. In that year Father Jacques Marquette brought his refugee band of Huron Indians to the secluded safety of Mackinac Island.

An agriculturally-based people, the Huron found the thin soil of Mackinac Island unsuitable for their crops. A year after settling on Mackinac Island, Marquette and his band of Hurons moved to the more fertile land on the north shore of the Straits. Here, Marquette and Father Claude Dablon founded the permanent mission of St. Ignatius Loyola (today St. Ignace, Michigan), named in honor of the founder of the Jesuit order. Nearby, the Jesuits also established the mission of St. Francis Borgia to the Ottawa Indians, another agricultural tribe who planted corn fields on the St. Ignace peninsula.

A fur trade community developed adjacent to the missions and by 1690 soldiers constructed Fort Du Buade to protect French commercial interests. As the trade grew, Jesuit priests found themselves competing for the souls of the native people with traders offering beads, blankets and brandy. When the French military closed Fort Du Buade and later reestablished a Great Lakes presence at Detroit in 1701, the Huron from St. Ignace migrated south and became the Detroit-area Wyandots. Left behind were the Jesuits and their faithful band of Ottawa still tilling the soil at the Straits of Mackinac. After depleting the soil at St. Ignace, the Ottawa and their Jesuit priests moved to the south shore of the Straits of Mackinac (today Mackinaw City, Michigan), sometime around 1708. In 1715 they were once again joined by French fur traders and soldiers who constructed the palisaded community of Michilimackinac.

The Jesuits soon found themselves ministering to both their Ottawa converts in the mission and the growing French-Canadian population in the adjacent community of Michilimackinac. Fulfilling their dual responsibility became more challenging for the Jesuits after 1741 when the Ottawa moved 20 miles south along the Lake Michigan shore to L'Arbre Croche where they established new crop fields. The Jesuits transferred their mission to L'Arbre Croche while continuing to serve the small but active Michilimackinac congregation. Now separated from the mission, the Michilimackinac congregation built a new church a few years later and named it "Ste. Anne's," in honor the mother of the Virgin Mary. The residents of Michilimackinac had a special devotion to Ste. Anne as she was the patron saint of voyageurs.

Despite the British conquest of Canada and occupation of Michilimackinac in 1761, the Church of Ste. Anne continued to flourish until Father Pierre DuJaunay was recalled four years later. The nearly unbroken presence of Jesuit missionaries in the Straits of Mackinac ended when DuJaunay closed the mission at L'Arbre Croche and left Michilimackinac in 1765. Shepherdless, the flock continued to practice their religion as best they could. The faithful gathered for public prayers in the church, kept private devotions in their homes, used lay leaders to perform sacraments and looked forward to the occasional visit of a missionary priest. Parish leaders cared for the church and adjacent priest's house – forever hopeful that a priest would return to their remote parish.

British authorities moved the Michilimackinac community to the safety of Mackinac Island during the American Revolution. Hoping to encourage the French-Canadian residents to move as well, Lieutenant Governor Patrick Sinclair ordered Ste. Anne's Church dismantled and taken to the island in 1780. The sturdy log church was rebuilt along the shore of the island's protected bay below the towering bluff that became home to the new fort.

The congregation repeatedly petitioned church authorities to send a permanent priest to Mackinac. Their poignant appeal to Bishop John Carroll of Baltimore in 1804 expressed their deep desire for priestly ministry: "The innocence of the children, the weakness of the aged, the sins of the most vicious, all these demand the favor of your pastoral charity...to forestall the sad results of a flock straying without a shepherd." A year earlier Father Gabriel Richard testified to the sad state of affairs at Mackinac when he learned that the church alter had been desecrated and the priest's house turned into a public brothel. In desperation, Richard recommended that the church ornaments, books, portable altar and chalice be sent to Detroit rather than be spoiled or abused by the community.

As church authorities sent only visiting clergy to Mackinac, it fell to the steadfast dedication of Ste. Anne's parishioners to sustain the parish through these difficult times. Magdelaine Laframboise, a prominent

Mackinac Island fur trader of mixed Ottawa and French blood, provided crucial leadership and support during the first half of the nineteenth century. Her devotion is well documented in the parish register where she frequently appears as a godmother to the baptized and witness at marriages. "Madame" Laframboise donated the property adjacent to her home when parish leaders decided to move the church and priest's house from their original location in the village to the current site on the east side of the island harbor in the mid 1820s. In exchange for her gift of land, Laframboise asked to be buried beneath the altar at the end of her life. Father Henri Van Renterghem honored her request when she died in 1846.

Father Otto Skolla's 1845 sketch of Ste. Anne's Church and priest's house on Mackinac Island. Magdelaine Laframboise's house is shown on the left.

In November 1830 Ste. Anne's parishioners warmly welcomed Father Samuel Mazzuchelli to Mackinac Island. A twenty-three-year old, Italian-born Dominican, Mazzuchelli was Ste. Anne's first resident priest since 1765. With Laframboise's assistance, Father Mazzuchelli started a Catholic school for island children. Martha Tanner, who spent much of her adult life teaching Indian and Metis children at Mackinac and L'Arbre Croche, joined Josephine Marly as the school's first teachers. Nearby, a Presbyterian mission under the direction of Reverend William Ferry likewise sought to attract young scholars to its classrooms. Conflict was inevitable. Although a flourishing fur trade attracted enough students for each school, Mazzuchelli and Ferry jealously guarded their congregations and competed to bring in new converts. Their antipathy climaxed in a series of theological debates in which both sides claimed minor victories.

In spite of the brief conflict between Mazzuchelli and Ferry, ecumenical cooperation often characterized the relationship of Mackinac Island's various denominations. Life on this remote and self-sufficient island required mutual respect and support if the parishes were to survive. It was the devout Catholic Magdelaine Laframboise, who first welcomed Reverend Ferry to Mackinac Island in 1823 and provided space in her home for his first classrooms. In 1840 Father Toussaint Santelli and a Methodist minister jointly conducted a worship service for soldiers at Fort Mackinac. Overwhelmed by the sight of "two such characters behind the same desk," Lieutenant John Phelps exclaimed "one would think that the time of the lying down of the lion and the lamb together had come."

Workmen tearing down the old log church in the early 1870s. (Photo credit: *Mackinac State Historic Parks*)

By the mid 1870s the small log church, first built at Michilimackinac and having survived two moves, was torn down. Parishioners replaced the simple log building with an imposing gothic structure that was more appropriate for the island's evolving image as a celebrated summer resort.

Since the end of the Civil War, Mackinac had been an increasingly popular "watering spot" for travelers, vacationers and health seekers. Federal authorities created Mackinac National Park on the island in 1875 and tourists packed north-bound steamboats and rail cars heading for Mackinac. The island's changing character was reflected in the pews at Ste. Anne's Church where summer tourists and curio merchants replaced the voyageurs and fur traders who worshipped on the same site fifty years earlier.

The success of the elegant Grand Hotel, constructed in 1887, propelled Mackinac Island to new fame and fortune. The hotel attracted a stylish and aristocratic clientele who christened Mackinac "the most fashionable" resort in the upper Great Lakes. Wealthy entrepreneurs from Chicago and Detroit, including the Cudahy brothers of meat-packing fame, constructed opulent "cottages" on the island's cedar-lined bluffs overlooking the Straits of Mackinac.

Parish leaders, deciding that their church was not in keeping with the island's fashionable character, conducted a major restoration and redecoration project beginning in 1890. Father Antoine Rezek started tentatively by purchasing new vestments and church linens, but soon made bold suggestions about replacing cracked plaster and redesigning the sanctuary. With his ideas accepted, workmen stripped the church to its studs and rebuilt the walls to their current configuration. The project was not inexpensive, and the parish elected to sell the old cemetery in town for $800 and transfer interments to the new burial ground in the center of the island. West Bluff cottagers John and Michael Cudahy each donated three hundred dollars. With additional gifts from parishioners and visitors, Father Rezek was able to leave the island in 1891 with the project completely paid for.

Interior of Ste. Anne's Church after 1890's restoration and remodeling. (Photo credit: *Mackinac State Historic Parks*)

Father James Miller continued Rezek's work by constructing the semi-circular steps in front of the church and remodeling the steeple. Father Miller added the fresco wall decorations and commissioned E. Hackner, a renowned altar builder, to construct three elegant white and gold altars. With the addition of new stained glass windows in 1912, the church assumed the general appearance that would carry her through the twentieth century.

The construction of basement in the mid 1950s provided the blessing of a parish hall but the curse of structural instability. The excavation had weakened the foundation and the side walls eventually began to sag while the plaster cracked. Perhaps it was the revenge of Madame Laframboise whose remains were removed from beneath the altar and reburied outside the church. Regardless, one hundred years after the 1890's stylish

Winter at Ste. Anne's Church

remodeling, the church was once again in need of substantial work. True to Mackinac Island's ecumenical heritage, a committed group of individuals from several denominations raised over one million dollars from Catholics, Protestants and Jews, year-round residents, summer cottagers and day tourists.

The 1990s restoration recaptures the 1890's appearance. The project has been completed as the parish celebrates its tri-centennial anniversary. This celebration is linked to the parish's earliest written records which date to 1695 and recalls the tremendous efforts of the Jesuit priests and brothers who first brought the message of Christianity to the shores of Mackinac. In the following pages Brother Jim Boynton eloquently describes this remarkable chapter of Mackinac history. Brother Boynton reopens long-closed pages of Jesuit activity at Mackinac and brings to life the struggles and successes, disappointments and dedication of the priests and brothers who labored in the wilderness and planted the seeds of faith that flourish today.

Phil Porter
Mackinac State Historic Parks

Author's Preface

In 1971, as the City of St.Ignace celebrated its tri-centennial, I most likely was more taken with my fourth birthday, but my memories of the events are clear. Perhaps it was because my father played Father Henri Nouvel in the town pageant, or because my brother helped make the invitations sent to the governor and other important dignitaries. Even at that young age, however, I was fascinated with the history of the Straits area. What we commemorated that year was Father Jacques Marquette's landing on our shores and establishing a mission with the displaced Huron and local Algonquin tribes of Native Americans. His fame would come later with an exploration of the Mississippi, but clearly he was still "ours."

Yet Marquette was not alone, nor was he the first, last, or most important Jesuit to work in the Straits region. The Jesuits, as the Society of Jesus is known, played a major role for the first third of Mackinac's recorded history. The mission of *Saint Ignace de Missilimackinac*, named after the founder of the Jesuits, St. Ignatius Loyola, occupied a key position in exploration, evangelization, native linguistics, morality, and daily religious life for the vast percentage of the Native and European population. The many priests and an occasional brother of the Society of Jesus were more than just local or even Canadian figures. As part of an international Jesuit mission effort they were following the lead of Francis Xavier in India and Japan, as had Eusebio Kino in California and Arizona, John Carroll in Maryland, the Reductions of Paraguay, Roberto de Nobili and Cristóvão de Brito in India, Alessandro Valignano in Japan, and Matteo Ricci in China.

What these men were about and their "way of proceeding," a common expression of Ignatius in referring to the Jesuit mode of ministry and lifestyle,[1] always had a distinctive Jesuit flavor to it, but what they were about at the Straits of Mackinac warrants a chapter of its own. This is the story of these sons of St. Ignatius and those with whom they worked from 1670, when Claude Dablon first set foot on Mackinac Island, until 1765, when Pierre DuJaunay, forced by the political situation in Europe, witnessed the suppression of the French Jesuits.

In writing this, I am greatly aware that I have been helped and supported by more than the dead men who left behind their letters. My mother and father have put up with my Jesuit obsession for years, and I would like to thank them. Phil Porter, aside from writing an introduction and helping me in my research, has been a great mentor ever since 1985, when he first taught me to fire a musket. Fathers Robert Toupin, S.J. and Lucien

Campeau, S.J., from St.-Jérôme, Québec, were a great help in getting me started with the archives, and in deciphering ancient French script. Lewis Crusoe was a tremendous source of information, and Father Joe Daoust, S.J. is the reason this book holds more fact than fiction. I would like to thank my Jesuit community at Hopkins House, Cambridge, Massachusetts, and especially Tom Stegman, S.J., J. Michael Flynn, S.J., and Christopher Derby, S.J. They are all pardoned from reading this book because they have heard everything in it many times over. Valerie Porter designed the cover, and Father Jim Williams provided both financial and spiritual assistance. Christopher Daignault, S.S.E., spent a good deal of time translating the Latin texts, and he is not even *nostri*. Thanks to Brother Guy Consolmagno, S.J., who used his skills in astronomy to verify what his confreres had done years before. Kevin Amer was most likely scandalized at the amount of proofreading he had to do for his former teacher; Ray Guiao, S.J., Charles O'Byrne, S.J., and Karl Kiser, S.J. were just glad I wrote in English. Thanks to all of you for your many hours. Finally, I would like to thank my professor and thesis director, Father John O'Malley, S.J. Few students have had such a mentor.

Weston Jesuit School of Theology
Br. Jim Boynton, S.J.
Cambridge, Massachusetts

Chapter One: "...do not begin to paddle unless you are inclined to continue paddling"

-Jean de Brébeuf, S.J. 1637

No story of Jesuits anywhere is complete without a look at the man who started it all, St. Ignatius of Loyola. Iñigo de Loyola was born in Spain to Basque lower nobility in the year 1491, and at the age of sixteen he was sent to be a page of Juan Velasquez, Treasurer-General of King Ferdinand of Spain. Here he followed the life of a courtier and eventually became a soldier. Needless to say, his lifestyle often included the carousing and gallivanting typical of this occupation. In 1517 Iñigo joined the service of the Duke of Najera, who occupied the city of Pamplona on the border of France and the newly claimed Spanish Navarre. It was in defense of this city that Iñigo had his leg shattered by the French cannon. Sent back to Loyola castle for convalescence, he began the long road to recovery. During this time he dreamed of glorious deeds to perform when recuperated, and asked for books on chivalry. None found, he was offered *The Life of Christ* and *The Lives of the Saints*, and, in reading, began to question whether he too could perform deeds similar to those of Francis or Dominic. Once healed, Iñigo left Loyola castle and started his spiritual quest at the Benedictine monastery of Montserrat. In a night vigil he hung his sword at the altar of the Black Madonna and officially renounced his past ways. Then, at a cave in the nearby city of Manresa, Iñigo wrote the outline of his *Spiritual Exercises*, a thirty-day silent retreat, principally a series of meditations on the life of Christ, later to be taken by all Jesuits. Soon it became clear that while his spirituality was sound, he would need more education to continue his ministry of preaching and religious counseling. Thus began his delayed yet arduous education which would eventually lead him to the University of Paris. Here he gathered the nucleus of what was later to become the Society of Jesus. Among these was his roommate, Francis Xavier, one day to become the most noted Jesuit missionary. This early Parisian group professed vows of poverty, chastity, and a pilgrimage to the Holy Land. If the pilgrimage did not succeed, they would go to Rome and offer their services to the Pope. Wars on the Mediterranean cancelled their plans, and thus the group presented themselves in Rome, where on September 27, 1540, Pope Paul III approved the Society of Jesus.

This new order differed from others in that its members were primarily devoted to ministry, not secluded in a monastery. They would serve God by serving others. The vows of poverty and chastity kept them available and flexible, and a special vow to obey the Pope in regards to missions, put them at his disposal. Positions in the Church's hierarchy such as Bishop and Cardinal were to be eschewed, and lastly, they would not chant the Divine Office in common as all other orders did. The formation of scholastics, those members heading towards priestly ordination, was also to be more rigorous than had been the norm. Usually the Jesuit course of studies would take around 12 years to achieve ordination, with an additional year of spiritual formation before final vows. In this lengthy process the young man would experience the *Spiritual Exercises*, study the liberal arts, natural sciences, and philosophy, followed by a period known as regency, when the scholastic would generally teach in one of the schools run by the Society of Jesus. With this phase completed came the study of theology, which led to priesthood. Brothers, the lay members of the order referred to as *temporal coadjutors*, also took the *Exercises*, but their formation varied depending upon need. Governance of the order relied heavily on openness and honesty with one's superior; provincials, who were appointed by the Jesuit curia in Rome, met yearly with individuals for them to give a complete interior self-disclosure. Ignatius became the first Father General, and through his written *Constitutions of the Society of Jesus* and guidance, the order soon grew to be an international affair.

"Loyola Renouncing the World." A painting of St. Ignatius Loyola by Mathaus Langus. Given to St. Ignatius Church, St. Ignace, Michigan by Father Frederic Baraga in 1837.

From the onset the new order was active in the mission field, in fact the fourth vow was a vow to be a missionary. The lead was given by Francis

Xavier, who traveled to India and Japan and died en route to China, but the main thrust was to follow. Similar to their educational system, the early Jesuits also had their own ideas about how one should go about spreading the Christian message. Perhaps the phrase which best sums up the Jesuit approach would be the Spanish proverb often quoted by Ignatius of "going in by their door in order to come out by ours."[2]   In other words, a Jesuit would use non-threatening methods to introduce himself to the target population. Once they have accepted him, (going in their door) he is then free to bring his message to the people (coming out his own door). With this idea in mind, the Jesuit would learn all he could about the language and culture of a people before introducing Christianity. Clear examples of this method can be seen in Roberto de Nobili, who worked within the Hindu system; or in Matteo Ricci, who went so far as to create Chinese religious rituals in communion with the Church of Rome. While this mode of evangelizing certainly proved effective, it was too far ahead of its time for Rome to accept, and as we will see, all Jesuit works were eventually suppressed by the papacy.

The support team for each mission was found in the curia of Father General at Rome, but also in the host province. Similar to the Franciscan and Dominican model, the Society of Jesus had also divided the world into geographical regions known as provinces. Obviously the hosts for the missions of New France were to be found in Old France, and here the Jesuits were into much more than just their missions across the sea. The Jesuits under Louis XIV held a sometimes troubled yet esteemed position in the royal court. François de la Chaize, S.J. was for thirty-four years the spiritual counselor to the King, while at the same time, tensions arose over loyalty to the Pope in what was to be known as the Gallican controversy. In a separate yet related controversy, the Jansenist movement accused the Jesuits of moral laxity and gave rise to Blaise Pascal's attack on the order in his biting series of correspondences known as *The Provincial Letters*. Education was also a top priority for the French Jesuits, and through their schools passed such men as René Descartes, the philosopher, and Molière, the dramatist.

The economic and political situation in New France was considerably different from that of the Old Country. Antoine-Denis Randot, a French intendant of Canada, makes the purpose of the colony abundantly clear in a letter of 1706 to the Comte de Pontchartrain in which he states, "Colonies are necessary only insofar as they are useful to the founding states; they are only useful if they procure these states with new benefits and assured means of increasing commerce."[3]   Old World culture was considered by Europeans to be far superior to anything existing elsewhere. While this is a matter of opinion, Europe was certainly the most technologically advanced culture at the time. In any case, an effort was made early on to try to transplant the European lifestyle to the unrefined Americas. The simple name *Nouvelle France* speaks volumes and seems to be in accordance with the perceptions of Thiery Beschefer, S.J., who in 1666 wrote, "Time only is needed to make New France like Old France."[4] True enough, this may have been a goal of the French, but during the time-frame of the Mackinac Jesuits, moves towards this vision were not as fast as one might think.

Royal control played a great role in New France, restricting colonization to those of unquestionable loyalty to the King. This, of course, excluded the large merchant class of Huguenot Protestants,[5] and actually led to a shortage of private individuals who could invest in the adventure. The effect was explained in 1732 by Gilles Hocquart, who wrote to the French government, "It would be desirable to have wealthy merchants in this country... they would be in a position to begin and develop enterprises..."[6] The French government did spend much money on the development of their colonies, but the market was never opened for private individuals as was done with their English neighbors. By the time the two empires were at war with each other in the 1750's, the British population in America was approximately one and a half million,[7] while the French population was less than 25,000,[8] even though they had more than twice the land.

Upon landing on American shores, Europeans were faced with many new experiences. Untamed land of this magnitude had not existed in Europe since before the Roman Empire, nor had peoples so untutored by continental standards. Europeans, who saw themselves as the center of the world, had a difficult time explaining where people native to the American continent had come from. Many theories were proposed, and William Penn even believed that the Native Americans had descended from the Ten Lost Tribes of Israel.[9]

Today we know that the first Americans came from Asia more than 20,000 years ago. Originally coming across the Bering Strait following animals they hunted, they eventually spread throughout the entire Western Hemisphere. In French territory were the Algonquin tribes, which consisted of the Odawa or Ottawa, Ojibway or Chippewa, and the Potawatomi. The Hurons, who were distant relatives of the Iroquois, also occupied land claimed by France. Although these peoples all engaged themselves in hunting, fishing, gathering and farming, the Odawa and Huron tended to be agriculturally based and less nomadic than the Ojibway whose traveled seasonally for their subsistence. Trading was a way of life among tribes. So vast were their trading routes that when Europeans landed on the East Coast, natives had with them copper from Michigan's Upper Peninsula and pipestone from Minnesota. Inter-tribal wars created fierce enemies within the Native American community, and many tribes would not begin to unite in any great extent until European oppression would give them a common cause. At the Straits of Mackinac this was seen most clearly in Pontiac's Uprising. In this rebellion, which took place, in part, at Michilimackinac, more than eight tribes joined forces in an unprecedented act against the British.

Whether the Europeans were French, English, Spanish, Dutch, or Portuguese, there is no doubt they thought of their culture as far superior to that of any non-Christian people. On the other hand, while a Native American might like certain material objects from European Civilization, there was little attraction to the lifestyle itself. Each culture shared feelings of fear, mistrust, superiority, unfamiliarity, and awe toward the other. With the arrival of the Europeans came many new things: animals, weapons, clothing, jewelry, religion, and disease. This caused tremendous shock. Natives had no idea how to react to these strange people. Europeans were at first looked upon as demi-gods who were sacred and powerful.[10] How else could a primitive mind explain people who brought disease yet did not die from it themselves, or who had such magical scientific equipment? After the initial shock, Natives immediately sought to trade for European goods and were willing to exchange food stuffs and to offer aids in survival.

Primary reactions to Native Americans by the French were similar to other colonizers' with only slight differences. Frenchmen tended to treat Natives as children, yet often with respect. Opportunities for trade and missionary activity filled Frenchmen with optimism towards the new relationship. It is true that the French came to make money, but they came in fewer numbers and with different attitudes than their English neighbors. Frenchmen sought a give-and-take relationship with Natives. They lived close to them and at times protected them from other opposing tribes, Europeans, or even individual Frenchmen. Another great gift to the Native population, at least in the French eyes, was something held very dear, Roman Catholicism.

Although Frenchmen usually thought of themselves as superior to Natives, this notion did not physically separate them. Relationships were established early on, and many marriages occurred between French *voyageurs* and Native women. Half-breeds or *métis* emerged, and soon became an accepted term, even if not always complimentary. This activity took place not only in lower classes; even Count Frontenac, the governor of

New France, adopted Native children and sent them to school. While this shows that he may have thought more highly of a European upbringing, he certainly felt the children were worthy of it.

French trade became very important to the Natives. A formal trading relationship was made with the Hurons in 1616 and continued for many years, benefiting both sides.[11] French wars greatly changed the Huron way of life, but unlike other tribes, the Hurons did not develop a strong dependance on European goods.[12] The French economy in North America revolved around the fur trade, and trading posts were spread throughout New France.

The fur trade remained the main source of income and continued to increase in importance. Individual traders often cheated, but not to the extent found in English trade, and fraud, while accepted, was never official policy. Trade was controlled by the government and ideally was enforced by clergy and military, and yet at Mackinac, the two often conflicted. As early as 1678, government officials assembled at Château St. Louis de Québec to limit the amount of alcohol that could be given to Natives, and Bishop François de Laval threatened to excommunicate those guilty of violating this practice.[13] Frenchmen did farm, fish for codfish, and engage in other business, but the fur trade remained essential, and this revolved around Native assistance.

Undoubtedly, not all was pleasant for Native Americans with the advent of French colonization in the first decade of the 17th century, and much damage was done to their culture. European disease, to which a Native had no immunities, wiped out entire tribes. Alliances divided Natives more than they had been and led to inter-tribal warfare. Starting in 1643 the French often held all-out war against the Iroquois, and thus drove them even more into British arms. Peace was attempted in 1666, and finally achieved in 1701. French technology began a rapid decline in Native crafts, and Catholicism ended age old beliefs, dividing tribes into factions.

Possibly the most influential French group among the Natives was the Society of Jesus. The first Jesuits to arrive in New France were Fathers Pierre Biard and Enemond Massé, in the spring of 1611. Upon their landing in Acadia, they were persecuted by the English and returned to France three years later. Not to be outdone, Massé returned to the colonies in 1625 as part of a team of three fathers and two brothers. They were met by the Recollect Franciscans, at whose house they temporarily lodged. In time, the order became established in Québec, and even though they founded a college, their main aspiration was to work among the Native population. The Jesuits frequently acted as an extension of the French Government and were given a monopoly on missionary endeavors early in the history of New France. This relationship is clearly seen in an introductory speech given by Samuel de Champlain in 1633. Here Champlain, in presenting the missionaries Brébeuf, Daniel, and Davost to sixty Huron chiefs and their companions, stated, "These are our Fathers. We love them more than our children or ourselves; they are held in high esteem in France; it is neither hunger nor want that brings them to this country; they do not come to see you for your property or your furs... If you love the French people as you say you do, then love these Fathers; honor them and they will teach you the way to heaven."[14]

In their official government roles, Jesuits explored interior America, sending to France reports and maps of what they found. They kept detailed accounts of trade and tried to protect Natives from undesirable European influence. The Jesuits were up front about their political capacity, knowing that if France prospered, their faith did too.[15] In this spirit, the Society of Jesus was a great aid in informing France about what it owned in the Americas and in extending its claims.

Jesuits acted as extensions of the Government primarily to help promote their faith. Natives were seen as a people desperately in need of the Church's teaching, and Jesuits aimed to fill that gap. What is interesting to note is the unusual attitude of these men who came from the center of European civilization. The Jesuit missionary mastered the Native languages and spent years learning their ways. In his directives for the missions, Jean de Brébeuf, S.J., unlike his contemporaries of other denominations, such as Reverend John Eliot of Massachusetts, instructs the evangelizers and not the evangelized.[16] First and foremost, he felt those who were to labor with the Hurons, "must have sincere affection for the savages,... looking upon them as... our Brethren with whom we are to pass the rest of our lives."[17] He continues in his instructions to show genuine concern and respect for Huron culture and hoped to prevent any possible *faux pas* by a well-meaning missionary. While he must have thought higher of his own society, Brébeuf's goal was converting people to Christianity and not to European ways, and he retained much of the Huron culture. Efforts were made to present Christianity in an understandable manner, as is shown in his famous "Huron Christmas Carol," and the converts were numerous. Brébeuf felt that the Jesuits' success could only be achieved if they were willing to leave their philosophy and theology behind and enter into another world.

As mentioned above, the French waged war against the traditional enemies of the Hurons, the Iroquois. It was at the latter's hands that Brébeuf eventually met his death, which has been hailed as martyrdom by the Church and popularized by North American Catholic piety. The terrible tortures he suffered were only a precursor to the later defeats of the Huron. It was during this inter-tribal war, dominated by the Iroquois, that the Jesuits followed fleeing tribes into the territory of the Upper Great Lakes. By 1668 Father Claude Allouez had migrated with a group of Hurons to the Eastern shore of Lake Superior, near Ashland Wisconsin, and Brother "Little Louis" Le Bœsme and Father Jacques Marquette worked with the Natives of Sault Ste. Marie. The mission at the Sault had a long history that went back to the time of St. Isaac Jogues. Eventually it became the geographic center from where the French military officer, Sieur de Saint-Lusson, claimed all the lands of the Great Lakes region for the King of France in 1670.[18]

Chapter Two:" Missilimakinac... The Key and the Door... "

-Claude Dablon, S.J. 1670

Father Claude Dablon, the superior of the Jesuit community at Sault Ste. Marie, believed he had found the ideal location for the newest mission under his charge, and in 1670 he wrote:

> Missilimakinac is an Island of note in these regions. It is a league in diameter, and has such high, steep rocks in some places that it can be seen at a distance of more than twelve leagues.
>
> It is situated exactly in the strait connecting the Lake of the Hurons and that of the Ilinois, and forms the key and the door, so to speak, for all the peoples of the South, as does the Sault for those of the North; for in these regions there are only those two passages by water for very many Nations, who must seek one or the other of the two if they wish to visit the French settlements.
>
> This circumstance makes it very easy both to instruct these poor people when they pass, and to gain ready access to their countries.
>
> This spot is the most noted in all these regions for its abundance of fish, since, in Savage parlance, this is its native country. No other place, however it may abound in fish, is properly its abode, which is only in the neighborhood of Missilimakinac.
>
> In fact, besides the fish common to all the other Nations, as the herring, carp, pike, golden fish, whitefish, and sturgeon, there are here found three kinds of trout: one, the common kind; the second, larger, being three feet in length and one in width; and the third, monstrous, for no other word expresses it,--being moreover so fat that the Savages, who delight in grease, have difficulty in eating it. Now they are so abundant that one man will pierce with his javelin as many as 40 or 50, under the ice, in three hours' time.[sic][19]

This would not be the first time that Mackinac Island was to be inhabited by Natives, nor even by the same Huron tribe which was coming, but the road leading to Father Dablon's plans of 1670 was a winding one. As mentioned, inter-tribal warfare existed, and among the most feared tribes were the Iroquois, who had driven the Christian Hurons from their homelands in the 1650's. There had been a time when the Hurons inhabited the Mackinac region, but again fear of the Iroquois had forced them to flee. At the period of Father Dablon's first visit to the Island, a group of these displaced Hurons was living among the Ottawa at the Mission of Saint-Esprit, on the banks of Lake Superior in Sioux territory. Father Jacques Marquette, their pastor, aware that tensions were brewing with their hosts, hoped to move to some vicinity near the Sault.

Jacques Marquette was born in Laon France in the year 1637, and joined the Champagne Province of Society of Jesus at the age of seventeen.

His course of studies called for him to undertake his novitiate (the first two years of Jesuit training) in Nancy, a teaching stint at Auxerre, and philosophy at the Jesuit University of Pont-à-Mousson; his regency saw him at the cathedral city of Reims, and he was eventually ordained a priest in Toul. It is clear from existing correspondence that Jacques Marquette had always wanted to serve in the missions and gives this desire as his reason for joining the Jesuits. Even while still in training, the young scholastic wrote to Father General Giovanni Paolo Oliva from whom he received the response:

> I do indeed praise the zeal with which, as you say, you are borne towards the foreign missions, especially those of the Indies, where you will devote yourself whole-heartedly to the conversion of the barbarians. But as you have finished only physics, you shall have to wait until you complete a course in theology. Meantime cherish so ardent and holy a desire and be mindful in your holy prayers of Rome.[20]

Later, in a letter returned to the General, Marquette gives us a brief autobiographical sketch in stating:

> ... The petition is to the effect that your Paternity order me to set out for foreign nations [the foreign missions], of which I have been thinking from my earliest boyhood and the first light of reason so that I wanted to be off for them before I knew [anything about them]. ...That was my chief motive for entering the Society. I may add, besides, that formerly I had a preference for the Indies but at present am perfectly ready to go to any region at all to which it will please your Paternity to assign me...[21]

His wish was fulfilled, and on the 20th of September, 1666, the young priest found himself on the shores of New France. After an introduction to the colonies at Québec, Father Marquette spent time at Three Rivers, where he immersed himself in the Algonquin Language. His brief introduction soon ended; he was then stationed at Sault Ste. Marie, where he, Brother "Little Louis" Le Bœsme, and Father Claude Allouez spent the winter among the Chippewa. It was in the Sault that Marquette's interest in the "Great River to the West" was piqued by a visiting Shawnee who spoke of "the South Sea, from which his village was distant only five days--near a great river which, coming from the Islinois, discharged its waters into that sea."[sic][22] During this era of geographical ignorance, hopes were high for a water route to the West, which would increase trade for the French and greatly increase the mission field for the Jesuits. In time, Father Marquette was put in more frequent contact with people who knew of this river. This association began in 1669, when he replaced Father Allouez at the Mission of Saint-Esprit, where, in Sioux territory near the western shores of Lake Superior, he ministered to both the Chippewa and the long Catholic Huron.

Here he improved his rudimentary Huron language, worked at making inroads among the Ottawa, and gained a great deal of geographical knowledge. As a result of befriending and baptizing an Ottawa, Father Marquette was presented with an Illinois slave from whom he learned a good deal.[23] The lad introduced him to the languages of the West and filled his head with ideas of travel. Thoughts of expanding New France for God and King never left his mind, even when times at Saint-Esprit became tense.

The adversity which existed between tribes often dictated where a people lived, as was the case with the Hurons on the shores of Lake Superior. Hurons had long been fleeing their old nemesis, the Iroquois, and now, along with the Ottawa, they were living in Sioux territory. This tenuous situation was aggravated when Huron and Ottawa braves, breaking a solemn calumet ceremony of peace, had caused blood to be shed by the Sioux.[24] The situation seemed only to worsen, and Father Marquette, along with his superiors, felt it best to remove the Christian Natives from exposure to danger and pagan influence. Thus the Western exploration was put on hold, and Father Marquette was to accompany a migration to safer locations near Sault Ste. Marie.

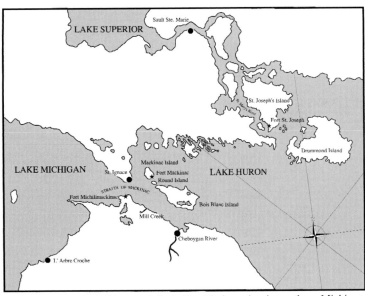

Map of Straits of Mackinac and Sault Ste. Marie region in northern Michigan (Photo credit: *Mackinac State Historic Parks*)

The task of finding the new mission site fell upon Father Claude Dablon, who at the time was superior at the Sault. Dablon was born in 1619 in Dieppe, a city with long association to overseas and missionary activity. He joined the Society of Jesus in Paris at twenty years of age and did the majority of his religious formation at La Flèche, a major Jesuit school. After ordination he was given a brief assignment before being sent to the missions in New France in 1655. Soon upon arrival, he was sent with Father Pierre Chaumonot to live among the Onondaga Iroquois, where Father Isaac Jogues had met a martyr's fate not long before. While not being fluent in their tongue, Father Dablon was able to charm the Natives with his musical ability, and Father Chaumonot used this to his benefit. This method was often used in the Jesuit Reductions of Paraguay with success, and the Iroquois' reaction to a "wood that speaks and is able to repeat what our children have said" was also positive.[25] During his tenure in the mission field, Dablon faced his share of danger among the Iroquois and also covered a great deal of the territory claimed by France. His written reports clearly show that of an experienced mission hand.[26] From the Jesuit College in Quebec Father Dablon was appointed superior of the Sault Ste. Marie Mission, and it was from here that he set off to find a refuge for those Christians who, indirectly through Marquette, were under his pastoral care.

A reconstructed bark-covered wigwam on Mackinac Island, similar to one used as a chapel by Father Marquette in 1670-71. (Photo credit: *Mackinac State Historic Parks*)

During the winter of 1670-71, Father Dablon "wintered here [Mackinac Island] in order to form plans for the Mission of Saint Ignace," and, declaring the place fit, he left in early spring.[27] True enough, Dablon recognized some disadvantages with the new location, such as the strong winds and movements of the water. His early departure, however, left him ignorant of the agricultural conditions on the limestone island. Thus when Marquette arrived with his refugees in the spring of 1671, all seemed to start off well for the new mission. Once the village was settled, a crop planted, and all was under way, Father Marquette left the mission to briefly return to the Sault, where he made his annual retreat and pronounced his final vows.[28] Coming from the spiritual high of his days in the Sault and excitement over the new mission, the young priest must have been disheartened to find the state of affairs on the island upon his return. In his absence it became obvious that the corn would not grow in the shallow soil, nor was there an abundance of game any larger than a rabbit in the small forest cut off by water. Therefore, in order to survive the coming winter, it was decided to move to the protected bay on the northern side of the straits. Undoubtedly, the transition must have been trying for a people so often dispersed, yet in the *Relation* of 1671-72, Father Dablon notes that Marquette "has not furnished us any special account of the occurrences at that Mission," and only continues to positively describe a people who, "In a word, observe all the exercises of piety that can be expected from a Christian body organized more than 20 years ago..."[29]

The following year the silence was broken, and Dablon's positive report is both echoed and enhanced by Marquette's own hand. His *Relation* of 1672-73 gives us a rare look at early life at the Straits of Mackinac and the very amicable bond between the Jesuit and Native peoples. The mission was well under way, and Marquette tells of a fort constructed near the chapel in which lived three hundred and eighty Hurons, who were "assiduous at prayer."[30] Even when Marquette was on retreat, he noted that "The Hurons came to the chapel during my absence, as assiduously as if I had been there, and the girls sang the hymns that they knew. They counted the days that passed after my departure, and continually asked when I was to return. I was absent only fourteen days; and, on my arrival, all proceeded to the chapel, to which many came expressly from their fields, although these were very far away."[31] Throughout the year, Marquette describes how he cheerfully attended their functions, such as the "festival of squashes," and took pleasure in hearing men of importance in the tribes proclaim themselves as Christians. He witnessed their dances and "did not find any harm in any of them" except one called the "bear dance." This particular masquerade was the desire of an impatient sick woman, and called for twenty women to dress, growl, eat, and act like bears, while the musicians struggled to perform bizarre music.[32] By and large, Father Marquette seemed to have a tolerance, if not respect, for much of the Native way of life, and he often wrote of their spiritual depth.

These first years in Saint Ignace were clearly those of a striving Christian community with a caring curate to shepherd them. Regular interchange occurred with the Natives coming to the chapel and Marquette going out to the fields to see his flock. He speaks of home visits bringing the Sacraments to the elderly, and mentions his admiration for a blind woman who had been instructed by Father Brébeuf, and still remembered her prayers after many years.[33] With the mission firmly established and a state of stability in inter-tribal affairs, the time finally seemed right for Marquette to pursue his goal of westward exploration. He informed Father Dablon, his superior, that he was getting ready to hand the post over to another's care in order to, under directive, "seek towards the south sea new nations that are unknown to us..."[34]

In harmony with the official position of Jean Talon, the first intendant of New France and a former pupil of Jesuit schools, the Society of Jesus also desired the expansion of French territory, and hoped for discovery of a river to the west. To carry out this task, Talon, along with Count de Frontenac, the governor, appointed Louis Jolliet during the summer of 1672, with the understanding that he would be accompanied by a Jesuit.[35] Jolliet was born in New France in 1645, and for a time pursued an ecclesiastical career and even received tonsure from Bishop Laval.[36] After five years in the seminary of Québec, Jolliet departed to eventually involve himself with the fur trade. He maintained good relations with the clergy, and his later work would bring him side by side with the Jesuits. Thus it was no surprise when, on December 8, 1672, the feast of the Immaculate Conception, Jolliet paddled into Moran Bay of Saint Ignace to meet up with his appointed companion for the expedition, Father Marquette. Marquette saw the possibility of spreading the word of Christ to the Illinois people, as well as those beyond, whom he had learned about back at Saint-Esprit. While the goals of the two men may not have been identical, the means to their ends were the same, and in the final analysis, both were clear on bringing glory to both the King of France and the King of Heaven.

By this time, Father Philippe Pierson, S.J. was on location to assume the care of the Saint Ignace Mission, and Marquette was free to leave. Meanwhile, the explorers took little time to ready themselves for the trip they had planned over the long course of winter. Thus, after an invocation to the Blessed Virgin, five men in two canoes filled with necessary supplies for cartography and record keeping, items for Sacramental life, Indian corn, and smoked meat, left the Mission of Saint Ignace de Michilimackinac on the 17th day of May, 1673.[37] With this exit Marquette began a journey that would change the face of America, yet he would not return to his mission of Saint Ignace alive. His travels, which set his name amongst the greatest

Father Pere Jacques Marquette, S.J.
(Photo credit: *The Department of Special Collections and University Archives, Marquette University*)

explorers of the New World, opened up much of the West for further settlement and successfully charted the Mississippi.[38] Unfortunately, the once robust Marquette began to be plagued with an intestinal disease, which came and went a number of times in its course.[39] Severely weakened by the disease, Marquette was headed back to Saint Ignace in May of 1675 when he died.

The account of Marquette's death in the *Relations* of 1673-77 reveal a man who was both saintly and well loved by his companions. In his piety he instructed his companions as to how they could assist him to death, and what they were to do with his remains. In this manner, often compared to St. Francis Xavier, the most prominent Jesuit to ever paddle the straits of Mackinac expired. Two years later, a group of Natives who had been instructed by Marquette at Saint-Esprit, finding themselves in the area of their pastor's grave, unearthed the remains, respectfully cured them according to their custom, and took them in solemn procession back to the mission of Saint Ignace.[40] Nearly 30 canoes of Iroquois and Algonquins paddled into the Straits of Mackinac and presented the remains to Fathers Pierson and Nouvel, who in turn celebrated the funeral mass and interred the remains in the middle of the church. Now buried at his former mission, Marquette's remains strengthened both the faith and devotion of the people he had loved so dearly.

Certainly Jacques Marquette was an able explorer, but more importantly he was, at the Straits of Mackinac, a loyal son of Ignatius. Animated by devotion to the Virgin Mary and strengthened by the *Spiritual Exercises,* Jacques Marquette of Laon France, according to his superiors, was "...all things to all men-- a French-man with the French, a Huron with the Hurons, and Algonquin with the Algonquins."[41] Yet after his death the importance of his settlement grew beyond that of an isolated Christian community, and what Marquette once took for granted, his successors would have to struggle to keep.

Late nineteenth-century view of Marquette's grave in St. Ignace, Michigan. (Photo credit: *Mackinac State Historic Parks*)

Chapter Three: "Captain Black Robe"
-slur to a Christian Kiskakon Chief, 1679

Upon his departure from the mission of Saint Ignace, Marquette was replaced by Fathers Philippe Pierson and Henri Nouvel, and it was they who received his remains from the Ottawa and Iroquois in June of 1677. These fathers had inherited a well-established mission, which eventually was so large that the assignment was split. Father Pierson ministered to the Huron at the original mission of Saint Ignace, and Father Nouvel established the Algonquins in a new location named in honor of the Jesuit, Francis Borgia,[42] three-quarters of a league away, near Gros Cap. Moreover, the seclusion of the post, at least in the early years, allowed the work to continue without much interference from a corrupting French influence.

Philippe Pierson was born in Ath, Hainaut in the year 1642, and at age eighteen he joined the novitiate of the Gallo-Belge Province located in Tournay. Seven years later he arrived in Québec, and was one of the first Scholastics to be ordained in New France. His superior at the Saint Ignace mission, Henri Nouvel, was born in 1621 at Pézenas, Hérault, and joined the Jesuit Province of Toulouse in 1648. After arrival in Québec, Nouvel spent time at the missions of Tadoussac and Sillery before being assigned superior of the Ottawa missions. For a decade both men labored among the Native population of Mackinac, and, except for the winter of 1675-76 when Nouvel traveled to Saginaw Bay, their time was generally spent together.

The first description of their work is found in a letter of Father Pierson, written from "Saint Ignace, at Missimilimakinac on Lake Huron, on the 25th of April, 1676." Here he states, "God has given up to the present, and still grants every day, so many blessings to my Huron mission of Tionontate, that I have the satisfaction of seeing this little church gradually increase in number and grow strong in faith."[43] He goes on to note that he passes over most noble actions in silence, only to state that the faith is becoming well-established, giving him much to be thankful for. He had achieved the cooperation of the medicine-men and jugglers, and the greatest threats to the mission were the attempts of the Iroquois to draw the Hurons into their wars and lure them out of the country.

The following years were ideal for the working of a Jesuit mission. Although there were French traders in the region, a presence which increased as time passed, their occasional contact with the Native population was not yet disruptive to the mission. As their confreres had done in Paraguay, the Jesuits at Mackinac worked with the indigenous population, in relative seclusion from outside European influence, to establish a truly Christian and Native community. The results seem quite favorable to all involved, and, with a total of about 1,800 souls, the mission became an important station, and the center for four distinct missions: those to the Ottawas and the Hurons at Mackinac, those to the tribes at the upper end of Lake Huron, and those to the Natives residing at Lake Nipissing.[44] In the year 1677, Father Jean Enjalran, who had been in New France less than a year, was sent to make an official visitation of the missions and to report back their conditions. He spent the year with Fathers Pierson and Nouvel, and his narrative to Father Dablon relates some of the most important insights we have of local Native and Christian activity.

As the mission was divided by tribal association, and the Hurons were older in the Faith, Enjalran commenced with them. Of these he notes their exacting practice of the Roman Catholic faith, and reveals that, true to the Jesuit way of proceeding, much of the leadership was held by the natives themselves.

> They hold in great respect the days assigned to prayer, as Sundays and feast-days, which they *especially* [scrupulously] observe. On those days the Christians and the Catechumens assemble very punctually, and in large numbers, in the church. There is a fervent Christian, who is a permanent officer, appointed to give notice of the days on which they are to meet; it is he, also, who addresses the meeting after the father has explained some point of our faith, and who fulfills, wonderfully well, the duty of preacher. He is commonly called 'the officer of the faith.' Besides this officer, there are two Christians who are quarterly officers; they have charge of all that concerns assembling for prayer, and are distinct from two others who are to say the prayer aloud in the church. It is impossible to witness anything more exact than the conduct of these officers, who come to the house three or four times to learn the hour when they are to perform their duties. They run through all the cabins to carry orders, and are very promptly obeyed.[45]

Father Enjalran also explains in the same report the method by which services and lessons were held. Mass, for which the Natives prepared the bread to be consecrated, was attended on the prescribed days, and special rituals of Benediction of the Blessed Sacrament and the Litany of the Saints were held on Saturday and Thursday evenings respectively. Catechumens and children had their own special programs, and scandalous folk were not admitted to the assembly. There were Jesuits at this time in China who created suspicion among religious authorities by celebrating Mass in the local vernacular language. The approach at Mackinac called for the "officers of faith" to lead singing while the uninterrupted exercise of devotion took place.[46] The Sacrament of Confession was practiced occasionally, but it was always given special significance on the feasts of All the Saints, Christmas, and Easter. Prayers for the exalted monarch of

France, Louis XIV, were never omitted from any act of devotion, and many times worship included antiphonal chant with local French inhabitants.

The liturgical year played an important role and added variety to their devotions. During Lent, aside from the usual devotions, additional services were held on Fridays, and penances, such as reduced entertainment, were practiced. As to the other Catholic practices of this season, Father Enjalran wrote, "I had much consolation in witnessing them venerate the Cross on Good Friday, and assist at all other holy ceremonies of that week with a spirit of devotion, visibly shown."[47] Their spontaneous prayer usually consisted of gratitude for their Christian faith, or for thanksgiving, such as with the first fruits of the harvest. The "festival of squashes," mentioned earlier by Marquette, is an obvious parallel to a contemporary American Thanksgiving, and included both feasting and a blessing of the crop.

Christmas was held in particular esteem among the Hurons, and their manner of celebrating this feast is a moving expression of Native piety. According to the continuing account of 1677, the children constructed a grotto, and one little girl took delight in fashioning sweet grass into a crib for the infant Jesus. The grotto was repeatedly visited, but even more importantly, was the focus of a grand celebration. The Hurons divided themselves into three groups, according to the nations that constituted the village, and were lead by three chiefs, each representing one of the magi from Christian tradition. These men, dressed in the finery of a king, and with offerings of porcelain and scepters in hand, conducted their company to the church. Under their crafted banners representing the Virgin and Child, and a portable star of Bethlehem, the congregation approached the grotto, where a wax image of the infant Jesus had been placed. Here they offered prayers before the procession, chanted the litanies, and returned to parade the symbol around their village. Following this ceremony, the Hurons invited the Algonquins to their homes, where a great feast was held. Later, non-Christians were also invited, and the merrymaking included traditional dances and entertainment. As if the above were not enough, the following week saw the same procession go across the frozen bay, where they were welcomed by the Algonquin settlement. Here another celebration took place, and afterwards one chief remarked that, "...by that feast, they all united as brothers to obey Jesus, and to entreat the divine child to preserve their children."[48]

Enjalran spent a good deal of time among the Algonquins, where he also described his perceptions. While he noted that the chiefs and the older people were nearly all baptized and made fervent profession of their faith, the children were the mainstay of the community. "The young boys and

21

girls who had been baptized were the most earnest and assiduous," wrote the priest, and "We heard them inviting one another to prayer..."[49] This provided the priests with entry into family life, and often led to the baptism of a sibling or parent. At times it appears that the priests would use whatever means possible to gain credibility. Once, at a later date, when the Algonquins were worshipping the Sun and the Moon, Fathers Enjalran and Bailloquet used their European measurements to predict an eclipse of the Sun.[50] Obviously, when it came to pass, more people were committed to the Jesuits' teachings. Moreover, like most Christians of the seventeenth century, Protestant and Catholic, the Jesuits were not beyond telling the Natives that God would wreak vengeance on those who offended him with false teachings. This spoke loudly to a people often struck with newly-introduced diseases. In spite of the Jesuits' efforts, it is clear that the Algonquin tribes had not matured in their faith as had the Hurons, yet they too had their chapel, and any description of the settlement only relates that of a striving Christian community.

Not everything at the missions of Saint Ignace was perfect; it was not a Garden of Eden. The Jesuits were often frustrated. At one point in his report, Enjalran wrote, "I will only add here that the sweet satisfaction which the missionary derives from these blessings that God gives to his labors is not without its bitterness and cross; there are still a great many heathens and libertines."[51] For the Natives, controversy and social stigma often accompanied conversion to Christianity. One Kiskakon Algonquin chief suffered the insults of his colleagues from Manitoulin, who said he was apathetic, and derogatorily referred to him as "Captain Black Robe."[52] Joseph Chikabiskisi, a devout Catholic Algonquin from a place referred to as *sable*, was observed to "make a loftier profession of Christianity notwithstanding the continual persecution to which those of his nation subject him."[53]

A more public and communal demonstration against Christianity was seen when a large cross was to be erected in the Algonquin village. When the notion to set up the cross was proposed at their council, a debate began as to what benefit it would be, or for that matter, of what use was prayer, the black robes, or the French in general? After some discussion, the Christian side won out, and construction was begun on the monument.

An unusual feature of the cross was the addition of the lance and sponge, depicting what was used to pierce the side of Christ. The non-Christians held that it represented an inevitable attack by the Iroquois, and the fact that Christ was going to hand them over. Moreover, it was pointed out that the Nadoissis, an enemy branch of the Sioux tribe, often crucified their prisoners and forced them to drink out of a bark vessel fastened to the end of a pole. This method of execution by the Sioux is, however, apparently unique. Nicolas Perrot in his *Mémoire* states that this tribe killed prisoners by shooting them with arrows.[54] Nonetheless, this situation did not bode well for all concerned, and another council was called. Here it was pointed out that the Hurons had erected a similar cross three years earlier with no ill effect, and that such a cross would please their allies, the French. Thus it was decided that the following Sunday, which happened to be Passion Sunday, all the Natives would go to honor the cross, a ceremony in which they had previously refused to take part. As the service began, with Father Nouvel vested in his surplice, and Christians, Catechumens, and others proceeding to the cross, a volley of musket fire was offered in salute. Chaos erupted when, as Enjalran wrote, "At the first volley, the sponge was struck with a ball; and at the second, the lance was thrown down, struck by two or three bullets."[55] Upon this action, the Jesuits retreated back to the chapel, and only a few of the most distinguished men from the nations were allowed inside.

Actually, this event seems to be a turning point, for within the very hour that the incident occurred, those responsible for the harm went out and fashioned another lance and sponge, and by dawn of the next day, all had been mended. The Natives expressed much remorse over the episode, and the following day, during a new attempt at dedication, the Chief of the Kiskakons voiced sorrow at their actions, and exhorted his followers to obey Jesus Christ and the fathers who are his spokesmen. Following this oration, the chief decorated the cross with porcelain collars, blessings were given, hymns were sung, and later, the nations "spoke conformably to what the chief had said, thanking him for the amends that he had just offered to Jesus Christ for all, and exhorting all in a similar manner to obedience and respect for the cross."[56]

On this positive note, Enjalran concluded his report on the mission at Mackinac; it certainly was not the end of activity. As time progressed, Mackinac became more than the focal point for Christian Natives and the occasional Frenchman. The late 1670's and early 1680's were a time of transition for the region, as it paradoxically grew more French and less Christian, at least in action. The same geographical prominence that had attracted Natives and missionaries to the straits area also applied to Frenchmen involved in the fur trade. Daniel de Greysolon du Lhut, after whom is named the present city of Duluth, Minnesota, was a frequent visiter to the Mackinac region for reasons of commerce. Following him were others with their mind set towards exploration, wealth, or both. By 1678 a military presence was established, and in August of the following year, the first sailing vessel on the Great Lakes, the *Griffin*, moored in Moran Bay. Aboard were Henri de Tonti, Father Louis Hennepin, a Recollect Franciscan, and René-Robert Cavelier, sieur de La Salle.

With the increased arrival of more and more Europeans, the role of the Jesuit began to change. Frenchmen, who were supposed to have been Christian for generations, were oftentimes very poor role-models to the Native neophytes, and Jesuits found themselves doing damage control. Furthermore, while the Society of Jesus had its strongest commitment to the Natives of the Mackinac Region, the French population rightfully looked upon the Jesuits' presence as in some way connected to them. In speaking of Sault Ste. Marie and Saint Ignace, the official narrative of LaSalle's voyages states, "In each of these places the Jesuits have a mission, not only for the sake of the Savages of the neighborhood, but because all those from the west or from the north who go to trade at Montreal must pass that way."[57] While this may have been true, the original intent, as seen in Dablon's plans, was to have a neutral location in relative safety.

In extreme cases, the Fathers at Mackinac had to act as peacekeepers. Henri de Tonti, who had charge over the crew of the *Griffin* during La Salle's absence, described the following event in a letter to Abbé Renaudot:

> ...On the 17th, [September, 1679] one of our men having been wounded by a Savage, I put our Frenchmen under arms to punish him who had done the deed and to put an end to the insults from these wretches. We marched to their fort and, as they were sallying forth with their weapons, we were about to fire upon them, when we perceived among them a Jesuit Father who was doing everything in his power to prevent what seemed about to take place. The chiefs of the nations came and asked my pardon, and the affair ended by their presenting me with some skins, saying that it was for a salve to the wound of the injured man.[58]

Incidents such as this may not have been commonplace, nevertheless the clash of cultures between Natives and Europeans often called for a moderator, and if a Jesuit could fit the bill, so much the better. Yet growing pains were not always the case for the mission; at times European contact must have been a welcome sight for the Jesuit community. When Duluth and Father Hennepin spent the winter of 1680-81 at Saint Ignace, the Franciscan wrote in his journal, "...Father Pierson and I would often divert ourselves on the ice, where we skated on the lake as they do in Holland. ...It is the usual diversion with which the inhabitants of [Ghent, Brussels-- and now Mackinac] entertain themselves during the Winter, by favor of the ice."[59] Clearly *Ora et Labora* was not perpetually followed by the vowed religious at Michilimackinac. Visitors traveling through would also have been a welcome sight, as they not only brought news from the outside, but also a chance to have intelligent conversation in French. Passing Jesuits were a regular sight on the guestmaster's list, and Henri Joutel of LaSalle's expedition wrote that Father Anastasius, a Recollect Franciscan, and LaSalle himself enjoyed the Jesuits' hospitality for the months of May and June, 1688. Joutel is quick to point out that he took up his lodging in "a little hovel some travellers had made."[60]

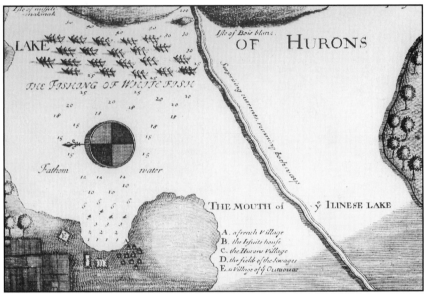

Baron Lahontan's 1688 map of the Straits of Mackinac.

Another noteworthy development with the arrival of more Europeans was that the missionaries' efforts could be evaluated by an outside party. Perhaps the outside reports were colored by the authors' own unfamiliarity with the inside of a church, but laymen did not often praise the Jesuits' missionary zeal or success. Joutel speaks of the Jesuits going to great length in translating to the Native tongues all things related to the Catholic faith, however he noted that, "there are very often none but a few women in their churches."[61] Baron de Lahontan, an officer under Count Frontenac, corresponded from *Missilimakinac* on May 16, 1688, and described the following:

> ...To the side of the Huron village, and enclosed in palisades, the reverend Jesuit Fathers have established their sacred space; it is the structure of a church connected to a college or house. ...These good apostles obsess themselves in making conversions, but I assure you, sir, that their work is in vain. The souls of the Savages are stubborn and inflexible, and there is no method by which they will learn the mysteries of faith. Practically all the

25

> fathers' efforts at establishing Christianity have resulted in the baptism of unknowing children, the old and decrepit, or those who at the point of death accept the Sacrament.[62]

These accounts certainly give another point of view, however the discrepancies might also be the very results of the authors' conduct and influence in the Native community.

The makeup of Saint Ignace drastically changed in 1685, when the area was made the military center of the Northwest, and the commandant of the garrison was invested with authority over all the French in the Mackinac country. Following this, a more permanent military base known as Fort deBuade was constructed to help oversee local operations. No longer were the Jesuits able to shepherd their Native flock in relative isolation. Moreover, they now had to compete with the growing secularization, which competed for the Native's souls. This tension was felt from the onset of the mission, but when a third wave of Jesuits arrived, and new leadership was appointed among the military, the conflict escalated to bitter disagreement.

Chapter Four: *"There is neither Divine nor human power that can permit the sale of this drink."*

-Étienne de Carheil, S.J., in a sermon at
Mackinac, 1697

Early in his tenure at Mackinac, Antoine de la Mothe Cadillac wrote a description of the village and garrison that he commanded. He told of the French post, Fort de Buade, and noted of the neighboring settlements that "The Jesuit residence, the French village, and those of the Hurons and Outaouas are adjoining to one another, and fenced together, they complete and fill the base of the harbor." He went on to observe that "The French houses are of wood, one piece on top of another, but they are roofed with cedar bark. There are none but those of the Jesuits that are roofed with planks."[63] By this time, Saint Ignace was a bustling town with a military presence of 200 soldiers, and many other French Canadian *habitants* who lived in sixty houses all in a straight street. The permanent Native American settlement numbered between six and seven thousand souls, and had cleared the land for three leagues around to cultivate corn.[64]

As the once-small mission grew, the Jesuits had to plan a strategy to keep the focus of their flock on Jesus. Similarly, as the opportunity for trade increased, the commandant of the garrison strove to promote the growth of this commerce. The main protagonists in this scene were Fathers Étienne de Carheil, S.J. and Joseph-Jacques Marest, S.J., who were opposed to the activities allowed by Antoine de la Mothe Cadillac. Each party was ardently loyal to both Church and Crown, but while one measured success in terms of docile converts, the other sought means of economic profit.

Father Carheil was born at Carentoir, France, in November 1633, and entered the Jesuit novitiate at Paris in 1653. He was ordained in 1666 and immediately departed for the missions of New France. Following preparation in Québec, he worked in the mission field among the Iroquois until hostile circumstances forced him to leave. In 1686 he was sent to work with the Hurons and Ottawas at Mackinac. His associate, Father Joseph Marest, was born near the cathedral city of Chartres, in Champagne, France, in 1653. He entered the Society of Jesus at age 18, and was followed ten years later by his brother, Pierre-Gabriel. Both men eventually came to the New World, but followed different paths. Indeed, during the time in which Gabriel was an English prisoner at Plymouth, his brother Joseph occupied himself with the mission of Saint Ignace.

Opposed to the Jesuits' efforts, stood the commandant of the outpost, Cadillac. He was born near Toulouse, France, around the year 1657, and joined the military at a young age. He arrived in America in 1683, and settled at Port Royal. In 1687 he married Thérèse Guyon, and together they had thirteen children. After some unlucky incursions by the English, in which he lost all of his property holdings, he received an appointment to the colonial troops by Count Frontenac, and went to the post at Michilimackinac.

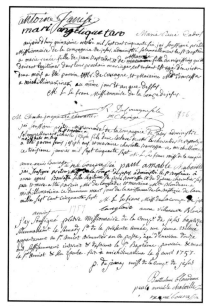
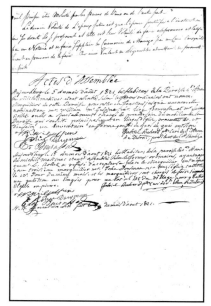

A page from St. Anne's parish register. The earliest entries date to 1695 when the Jesuit's were stationed at St. Ignace.

The Jesuits, long tired of watching their mission evolve from a temple into a den of thieves, called upon the law to fight the outside influences. The Church had fought the sale of alcohol with Bishop Laval's threat of excommunication, but now was the time to involve the Colonial Government. The Jesuits obtained an ordinance from the king to control the sale of alcohol, and by 1686 a special order was enacted that strictly limited the transportation of brandy to Mackinac.[65] The real conflict began when Cadillac was stationed in the Straits area from 1694 to 1697, during which time there was disagreement over how much authority he, as post commandant, had over the Jesuits. His personal interest in the fur trade, of which he was in control following 1705,[66] caused him to overlook abuses of the law about the brandy trade. In doing so, he managed to thoroughly anger the Jesuits, who did not hide their wrath. The animosity became personal, and Cadillac described Father Carheil as the most violent and seditious

28

person he had ever known. On one occasion Father Carheil accused Cadillac of not obeying the orders of the King or the precepts of God. Cadillac later wrote of the incident:

> I answered that this was seditious language that smelled to heaven, and I begged him to desist. Again he told me that I was not obeying the orders of the King, and that I was putting on airs, and at the same time he shook his fist under my nose. I tell you, Monsieur, that I almost forgot that he was a priest, and was on the point of breaking his jaw. But, thanks be to God, I contented myself with taking him by the arm, and leading him out of the fort, telling him to stay out of it in the future.[67]

Cadillac left Mackinac in 1697 and went to Quebec to make plans for his next venture, the establishment of a settlement called Detroit. While in Quebec, Cadillac felt he had the Jesuits' support in founding Detroit, even in spite of their difficult relationship at Saint Ignace.[68] However, once it became clear that the Recollects, and not the Jesuits, would staff the post, attitudes began to change. Finally, when groups of Natives began to relocate, and lawlessness started prevailing, the Jesuits bitterly opposed his efforts. The priests tried their best to curb the sale of liquor in Cadillac's absence, but were clearly fighting a losing battle. Father Carheil preached to his congregation in 1697 that "There is no power, divine or human, which could sanction the sale of this drink."[69] By this homily, the priest only managed to win the enmity of local Frenchmen, who accused him of going against the pope.

Cadillac had loftier goals in mind for Detroit than just irritating the Jesuits. He also hoped to put a check on English westward expansion and centralize French trade, but the Jesuits saw his endeavors as a plot against all that was just and good. Soon after the foundation of Detroit, Father Joseph Marest reminded Cadillac of Psalm 127, *Unless the Lord builds the house, those who build it labor in vain*, and told him that "[He could not] better aid the intentions of the king, who, in this kind of settlement which also concerns the savages, aims chiefly at the salvation of these poor souls, which the brandy traffic renders them incapable of."[70] Soon it became apparent, however, that the *eau de vie* would continue to flow, and that the settlement at Mackinac was descending into the law of the jungle. As a result, the Jesuits found themselves in desperate straits, and Father Carheil informed the successor to Count Frontenac, Governor Louis Hector de Callières, of the situation in a letter written from Michilimackinac in 1702. Here he states:

> ...The missions are reduced to such an extremity that we can no longer maintain them against an infinite multitude of evil acts--acts of brutality and violence; of injustice and impiety; of lewd and shameless conduct; of contempt and insults. To such acts the infamous and baleful trade in brandy

gives rise everywhere, among all the nations up here,--where it is carried on by going from village to village, and by roving over the lakes with a prodigious quantity of brandy in barrels, without any restraint. Had his Majesty but once seen what passes, both here and at Montreal, during the whole time while this wretched traffic goes on, I am sure that he would not for a moment hesitate, at the very first sight of it, to forbid it forever under the severest penalties...

...So much is this the case that all the villages of our savages are now only taverns, as regards drunkenness; and sodomies, as regards immorality--from which we must withdraw, and which we must abandon to the just anger and vengeance of God.[71]

After the initial unpleasant exchanges, a brief period of conciliation was attempted on the side of the Jesuits. Father Jean Mermet, from the mission of Saint Joseph, aspired to mediate between the two parties, and wrote to Cadillac stating "...you may see that the Jesuits are more friendly to you than you think, unless you yourself will not honor them with your kind remembrance, and if I dare say so, with your friendship."[72] Following this, Father Joseph Marest informed Cadillac that the missionaries were not trying to "hinder the settlement of [his] post, but to act for the best," and that they were "the servants of both God and of the King, and have no other interest which could induce [them] to act contrary."[73] Amicable relations were not to be, however, and the letter-writing campaign between Jesuit and governmental officials continued on.

Cadillac had grown tired of both the continuous correspondence, and the Jesuits' point of view on nearly everything. While he did allow the sale of liquor in Detroit, he also provided for the spiritual and educational needs of the Native and French inhabitants. For this task he relied on the Recollect Franciscans, even though they did not speak the Native languages.[74] Of the Jesuits, he wrote to Governor de Callières:

So large a volume could be made of all that the missionaries have said, preached, and written, since they have been in the lands of the Ottawa, against the trade in brandy and the [trading] expeditions in the woods that a man's [whole] life would not suffice to get through the reading of it...

...It seems that you wish that the Jesuits should be my friends. I wish it, too; but, as the quarrel dates from the time of the late Comte de Frontenac, and as they have very good memories, I must not think that they would forget the past, whatever I might do to attain that end, that that will not prevent me from having great regard for them, and much respect. All our quarrels have arisen only from the opposition they have offered to the orders of the King, which I know very well how to maintain, and to have carried out.[75]

The Jesuits at Mackinac continued in their persistence against the brandy trade, and against allowing the Christian Natives to relocate at Detroit. In May of 1703, Father Joseph Marest spoke of Natives who "had resolved to die at Michilimackinac, and that even if they left it, it would never be to go to Detroit..."[76] Yet by August of the same year, Cadillac felt he had the upper hand, and when a band of thirty Hurons from Mackinac arrived in Detroit, he wrote to Count Pontchartrain that, "Thus only about twenty-five of them [Hurons] remain at that place, where Father de Carheil, their missionary, remains ever resolute. This autumn I hope finally to tear this last feather from his wing; and I am convinced that this obstinate vicar will die in his parish without having a parishioner to bury him."[77] In encouraging the Natives to leave the mission at Mackinac, Cadillac thought of himself as taking on a holy quest, and even compared himself with Moses, who delivered his people from captivity.[78] He did, however, realize that he was taking on a formidable enemy, and stated that "...it would be better to sin against God, than against them [the Jesuits]. For on the one hand pardon is received for it, while, on the other, even a pretended offense is never forgiven in this world, and would perhaps never be so in the other if their influence there were as great as it is in this country."[79]

By 1706 the depopulation became so great that "the last feather was plucked," and, after burning their church and residence, the Jesuit Fathers returned to Quebec. Once there, the Court of Louis XIV induced the Jesuits to reinstate the mission.[80] The following year, Father Joseph Marest returned to the Straits of Mackinac, although, he most likely used the Southern "Mackinaw City" shore as his base of operations.

The real victims in this fluctuation were the Native Americans. By this time, their taste for alcohol was so strong that if they could not get it from the French, they had no qualms about going to the English. This trade distressed both Cadillac and the Jesuits; Cadillac saw French profits decreasing and the Jesuits saw the harm that alcohol was wreaking on the Natives. Moreover, many Native peoples had no desire or need to leave the Mackinac area. In the face of continued pressure from Detroit, the Ottawa presented their case to Governor Philip de Rigault, Marquis de Vaudreuil. In a speech delivered by the Ottawa in 1708, they informed the governor that "...although Monsieur de la Mothe [Cadillac] has sent to tell us to go to Detroit, we have no inclination to do so; we wish to dwell at Michilimakina."[sic][81] In response, the Marquis de Vaudreuil told them "...I put no restraint upon you in that matter, nor do I wish anyone whomsoever to restrain you."[82] Thus both sides had spoken on the matter, but official policy on Mackinac's position would not be determined for a few years.

The wounds inflicted on the mission by Cadillac's attempts to close it, the introduction of alcohol, and increased trade, were never fully healed.

Moreover, Mackinac's geographical prominence was not forgotten by those interested in the fur trade. The tension between the work of the Church and the aims of corrupt businessmen is often seen. In November of 1708, Sieur D'Aigremont visited the region only four days, but noted the following:

> ...it may be seen that Missilimakinac is the most advantageous post in Canada; and, to show its superiority over Detroit, I may tell you that even if all the savages in Canada were settled there we should not obtain one tenth of the quality of beaver pelts that we can get from Missilimakinac, for it would almost all go to the English by the agency of the Iroquois, the Hurons, and even many other savages who have gone that way...
> ...The day before I left Missilimakinac the Ottawa, who had gone down to Montreal arrived there. They brought more than five hogsheads of brandy, all got so drunk during the night that they set fire to their huts, seven of which were burned down; and they would all have been burned but for the French outlaws and my boatman, who ran and put out the fire. So intoxicated were the savages that they wanted to fight them, and prevent them from putting out the fire. The missionaries were also there, and they were likewise very badly treated and loaded with insults. No doubt, on the following nights, these savages burned the rest of their huts, and their fort, for they still had a great deal of brandy left. I assure you, My Lord, that the missionaries are in great danger at those times. These savages might have been prevented, at Montreal, from taking away such a large quantity of brandy.[83]

Observations such as this kept the issue of returning a military base to the Straits alive. Meanwhile, the difficult work of the Jesuits continued. That the Society of Jesus continued to minister to the local Natives seems certain, but in what fashion, and to what extent is unclear. In 1710 a traveling Jesuit, most likely Father Antoine Silvy, wrote from the post of *Michillimakina* and of the *Outavois*, that "As there are always Frenchmen among the savages, they have become more honest in their conversations and more docile in their manners; they always have a missionary."[84] Aside from tending to spiritual needs, the missionaries at Mackinac also acted as protectors for other Jesuits in danger, and as spokesmen for the Native population. In June of 1712, Father Joseph Marest welcomed Brother Louis-Pierre Haren and Father Jean-Baptiste Chardon into his home. They had fled their mission at Saint Joseph's River due to a war between the Ottawa and Potawotomi, and the Maskoutins.[85] Later that same summer, Marest informed the Marquis de Vaudreuil that the Native population, who had long desired a return of the French military, were growing impatient with their request.[86]

The Jesuit way of proceeding does not always call for a stable community, nor common prayer; however, the members often got together for retreats or formal visitations. In November of 1712, Father Joseph

Marest, the regional superior, was at the Mission of Saint Joseph. He was most likely there to offer support for the small community in the midst of their dangerous and violent situation. A week before he was to go, the mission station was visited by another voyaging Jesuit. The *Relation* of 1712 describes the surprise and joy felt when the two travelers each recognized the other to be his brother.[87] Joseph-Jacques and Pierre-Gabriel Marest had not seen each other in fifteen years, and had much catching up to do. Father Chardon offered his hospitality to the two, and together they finished out the week before heading together back up to Mackinac. During their trip of seventeen days up the Eastern shore of Lake Michigan, the two brothers enjoyed each other's company and profited from spiritual conversation. Gabriel was impressed with his brother's sanctity and dedication to his labors. He noted that the Natives had not taken to religion as a whole, but that there were a few souls who truly gave themselves to God. Of Joseph, he "wondered at the patience with which [he] bore [the Natives'] faults; at his gentleness, unwearied by their caprices and their coarseness; at his diligence in visiting and instructing them, and inspiring their indolent natures to activity in the services of Religion; and at his zeal and charity, sufficient to enkindle their hearts if they had been less hard and more compliant."[88] After two month's time, work forced the brothers to their difficult separation. Yet as they both believed that God had ordered their parting, so too would God temper its bitterness. This is a perfect example of the attitude cultivated by the vow formula of the Society of Jesus, which states, "...just as [God] gave me the grace to desire and offer this, so [God] will also bestow abundant grace to fulfill it."[89]

A military presence was reinstalled in 1715 by Constant Le Marchand de Lignery, which bolstered both trade and relations with local Native Americans. However, similar to the events a generation earlier with the establishment of Fort deBuade, the situation again became confusing for the Jesuits. Which populace, the French or Native American, was to be their primary concern? This tension is clearly seen in the account given by Father Pierre-François-Xavier Charlevoix, S.J. In the early 1720's, this priest, under royal commission, wrote a general description of his travels in North America. He visited Michilimackinac in June of 1721, and noted that "The fort is maintained, as well as the house of the missionaries, who are not at present terribly occupied. They have never found much docility among the Ottawa, but the court judges their presence necessary in a place where we must often negotiate with our allies. They also exercise their ministry for the French, who come here in great number."[90] At sixty-eight years old, Father Marest was still on location at Mackinac. The following year he was

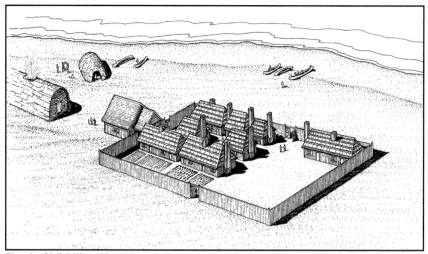

Sketch of Michilimackinac (Mackinaw City) as it appeared c. 1720 based on archaeological evidence. The mission church of St. Ignatius is attached to the west side of the palisaded fur-trade community and adjacent to the Ottawa village. (Photo credit: *Mackinac State Historic Parks*)

recalled to Montreal, and died in 1725. Marest's assistant at the time of Charlevoix's visit was Michel Guignas, S.J. He remained at Mackinac until 1727, at which time he went west to work with the Sioux.

Two years after Charlevoix wrote his description, Father Sébastien Rale, S.J. wrote a letter to his brother, in which he told of a winter spent at *Missilimakinak*. Father Rale observed that there were two Jesuits, one stationed with the Huron, and the other with the Ottawa.[91] He went on to explain the Ottawa religious beliefs with great understanding, but also with condescension. From the commencement of the Jesuit missions in New France, the emphasis was on the Native population over the French colonists. As Mackinac was a place where the two often merged, the Jesuits began to split their time between the two groups. The European names in the parish register indicate that this pattern would continue through the Jesuits' tenure and beyond.

Chapter Five: "...he is a very good man, and had a great deal to say... "

-Captain George Etherington, in regards to
Pierre-Luc DuJaunay, S.J. Michilimackinac, 1763

In the first half of the 18th century, the Straits of Mackinac again grew in military, economic, and religious prominence. Fort Michilimackinac became the military headquarters of the upper Great Lakes, and the village itself became an important link in the Montreal fur trade. The Jesuit mission became headquarters for the communities of Green Bay and Saint Joseph's River, and while the mission was not dependent on other Jesuit communities for support, continuous contact was also maintained with the brethren in Detroit. In 1735, Fathers Pierre-Luc DuJaunay and Jean-Baptiste de Saint-Pé arrived at the Mission of Saint Ignace de Michilimackinac. In the next thirty years, Father DuJaunay, along with other Brothers and Priests of the Society of Jesus, exercised considerable authority among the Native and European populations. Father DuJaunay's tenure established a separate mission for the Natives while continuing to minister to the Europeans. At a later date, he helped to usher in the peaceful change of regimes from French to English, and during Pontiac's Uprising, he exerted his influence to promote reconciliation and to save British captives.

Pierre-Luc DuJaunay was born on August 11th, 1704 (or August 10th, 1705), at Vannes, France, where as a youth he was a student at the Jesuit college. In 1723 he joined the Parisian Province of the Society of Jesus. His training included teaching grammar at his old Alma Mater, and later at Quimper, where he was a professor of humanities and rhetoric. Like many missionaries before him, he studied theology at LaFlèche and Paris, and following his priestly ordination in 1734, he sailed for New France. He came to Mackinac shortly after his arrival, where, with the exception of a few years at Saint Joseph, he spent the majority of his time in active ministry. The official Jesuit directories from Father DuJaunay's years at Mackinac have him listed as "among the Ottawa" and after his final vows in 1738, he is occasionally listed as the mission superior.[92] Even though most of his energies went to the Native peoples, he still devoted much of his time to the local European population and managed to keep up broader contacts and correspondence.

Jesuit training, community life, and ministry all create unifying experiences and tend to break down barriers and ease friendships. This is

The letters *IHS*, Greek shorthand for Jesus and used in the Jesuit seal, are carved into this catlanite pipe bowl found by archaeologists at Michilimackinac. (Photo credit: *Mackinac State Historic Parks*)

clear among those Jesuits who were stationed at Mackinac, but it also included the wider range of Jesuits working in the Great Lakes region, whom they could visit, as well as those Jesuits still in Europe, with whom they kept in touch by letter writing. Fathers DuJaunay, Jean-Baptiste de La Morinie, Marin-Louis Le Franc, and Claude-Godefroy Coquart, all of Michilimackinac, often traveled the Great Lakes to other missions as the need demanded, and did so to maintain contacts with other Jesuits. It is frequently noted that Father DuJaunay often visited Detroit, where his friend Father Pierre Potier, S.J. was stationed. In August of 1746 Father Potier wrote in his journal that Father DuJaunay came down to Bois Blanc Island where together they made their retreat.[93] A cheerful camaraderie existed, and in correspondence between Father Potier and other priests, they referred to Father DuJaunay as *Le Bec-Jaune*, or "Yellow Beak,"[94] a term of endearment. Their companionship endured over time, and when Father Potier died in 1781, seven letters from Father DuJaunay were found among his belongings.[95]

The friendships Father DuJaunay enjoyed from his remote mission station extended beyond his fellow Jesuits and included both religious sisters and laymen. An occasional trip to Quebec or Montreal helped to create and strengthen bonds made with the Ursuline sisters, and relationships formed with French businessmen and military officials who often passed through or lived at the Straits of Mackinac. Father DuJaunay wrote from Montreal to the Ursuline Sisters in Quebec during the spring of 1755, when they suffered a devastating fire. The sisters ran a girls' school, where they taught both Native and European children academics and household skills. "Though it is late, I would like to write a word of consolation," wrote the priest, and he went on to instruct the "suffering spouses of Jesus Christ... not to forget too much the spirit of poverty and its use."[96] Three months later, from Michilimackinac, Father DuJaunay wrote to the Superior, Mother Migeon de Bransac of the Nativity, and thanked her for gifts she had sent to his church, and informed her of the latest news from the interior wilderness.[97] For the parish at Michilimackinac, the Ursulines had embroidered *Dilectus meus mihi et ego illi* ("My beloved to me and myself to him") on a pall.[98] Aside from thanking the sisters for the gift, Father DuJaunay expressed his regret at their loss from the fire, offered some spiritual consolation, and gave them his latest news on the brewing French and Indian War (the struggle between France and England for the colonies). The sisters were informed that Michilimackinac was enjoying "...all the sweetness of peace and even the pleasures of triumph that our Ottawas, not without good reason, are boasted to have brought about at Fort DuQuêne."[99] He related that on July 9th, Monsieur de Beau-jeu, who died because of his excessive bravery, lead fewer than 800 men to defeat an opposing force of more than 3,000. He did realize, however, that the peace was tentative and could change given the critical situation of the colonies. In the letter, Father DuJaunay sent the regards of Madame DuMuy. The DuMuy family, often mentioned in the parish register, had a relative in the Ursuline convent by the name of Mother DuMuy of St. Helen. In conclusion, he asked for the sisters' prayers, and assured them of his. So deep had the relationship grown between Father DuJaunay and the Ursulines that after leaving Michilimackinac in 1765, he lived at their convent and served as the house confessor.

As in all French Canadian settlements of the time, the local parish was the spiritual, social, and physical center of the community. Weddings, funerals, and baptisms were held as needed, and mass and confession were offered on a regular basis. Between the years 1742 to 1765, Father DuJaunay performed 25 weddings and 120 baptisms among the European community,[100] an amazing number when one realizes that the population was at times as low as 200, and that a sizeable proportion of it included military personnel. Like most human organizations, the Catholic community at Michilimackinac included those members who took active and supporting roles, those who were casual participants, and those who bitterly opposed the work of the congregation and the Jesuits. The parish had an administrative council, composed of elected laymen who, together with the pastor, were known as the *fabrique*. This organization administered the temporal affairs of the church, rectory, cemetery, etc. Accounts still exist from the spring of 1764 which give the financial status of the *fabrique* at Michilimackinac. The small amount of 345 livres remained in the funds at this time.[101] Individual members of this council were named *marguilliers*, and were obvious leaders in the community. In an entry from February 4th, 1756, Ste. Anne's baptismal register records the godfather of the one baptized as, "Mr. Langlade,--the *Marguillier* of this parish."

The Langlade family was active in the parish and worked closely with the Jesuits. Between 1743 and 1760, Augustin de Langlade appears seventeen times in the parish register as a witness in certificates of marriage, and twenty-three times as a godfather. The family was engaged in the fur trade, and consequently settled at Michilimackinac. Augustin was married to the sister of the principal leader of the Ottawas, Chief Nissaouakouad, or as the French called him, *LaFourche* ("The Fork"), and this relationship gave both him and his son, Charles, high standing in the Ottawa nation. Charles was born at Mackinac in early May of 1729, and was baptized on the ninth day of that month. His childhood education was beyond what most would call typical. From his mother and uncle, he learned the customs of the Ottawa; from his father, he learned the ways of business; and from Father DuJaunay, the lad obtained an academic background required of any cultured Frenchman. Charles' marriage to Charlotte Ambroisine Bourassa took place at Michilimackinac on the 12th of August, 1754, in a ceremony witnessed by Father LeFranc, who also baptized their first daughter the following year. Charles Langlade went on to pursue a military career in the French army and was present at the defeat of General George Braddock and George Washington in Pennsylvania (an account earlier related to the Ursuline Sisters by Father DuJaunay), as well as at the defeat of the Marquis de Montcalm on the Plains of Abraham in Quebec. In 1761, Langlade turned over the Post of Michilimackinac to the British, and during Pontiac's Uprising, both he and Father DuJaunay aided the British captives and tried to maintain peace. Langlade later served the British during the American Revolution, and he died in Wisconsin sometime after 1801.

Parish administration and personalities were difficult at times, and involved a broader scope of people than just the *fabrique*. The case of

Joseph Jean-Baptiste Amiot-Vincelot is a perfect example of this sort of unpleasant affair. Monsieur Amiot was employed by the parish as the village blacksmith and was apparently unsatisfied with his conditions. Perhaps through the influence of his Native American wife, Marie-Anne, Amiot was able to get Chief LaFourche to argue on his behalf to Monsieur le Marquis de Beauharnois, the Governor-General of New France. In a speech given at Montreal on June 16th, 1742, LaFourche stated:

> My Father, for fifteen years one Amiot, married to a Sakise, has been settled at Missilimakinac working at his trade of armorer and blacksmith with the Jesuit Fathers, who keep back from him one half the proceeds of his labor. This makes it impossible for him to provide for the subsistence of his wife and eight children, whom we have to support, as they come to our cabins every day for food. He wanted to leave the post and go to the Illinois. We urged him to remain, telling him that you would be good enough to free him from his work. We trust, My Father, that you will not refuse this request.[102]

One week later, hoping to keep the peace, Monsieur de Beauharnois addressed LaFourche and his band with the following words:

> My Children, I have carefully considered the representation you have made to me with reference to one Amiot, a blacksmith. I have entered into his trouble and into yours. I have consequently given my orders to Monsieur de Vercheres. You will have reason to be satisfied with the arrangement I have made.[103]

Whatever the arrangement was, Monsieur Beauharnois explained to the French Minister in October of 1742 that there were two blacksmiths at Missilimakinac. One belonged to the missionary and was remunerated with four hundred livres and a few pots of brandy. The rest of his profits went to the priest. The other blacksmith had been removed from his duties five years earlier when the missionary had taken all of his tools away. The Commandant, Sieur de Celoron, reinstated him, and even though half of his profits still went to the parish, the priest was unhappy with the situation.[104] The following year, Father DuJaunay helped his other blacksmith, Pascal Soulard, in attaining a land grant, and of Soulard's character he wrote, "I sincerely like [him]."[105] Jean-Baptiste Amiot moved to Green Bay, where he was killed by a Native American. It seems that Amiot refused to return a repaired hatchet to a man named Ishquaketa, and later burned the Native with hot tongs in an ensuing argument. Ishquaketa's brother took revenge with a knife.[106]

The blessings and trials of working with the European community at Michilimackinac played a secondary role to the Jesuits' primary occupation of ministering to the Native Americans. Father DuJaunay's efforts with the Ottawa people is clearly evident in a series of letters known as "The

Aulneau Collection." Father Jean-Pierre Aulneau was a French Jesuit who was killed by a Native American at Lake of the Woods in 1736. Following his death, Father Aulneau's mother maintained correspondence with many of her son's friends, including Father DuJaunay. In September of 1739, Father DuJaunay wrote Madame Aulneau and asked for her prayers for the "forlorn tribes committed to my care."[107] He went on to express his desire that the tribes would settle down in order to be more easily brought to the faith. Until that time he could only hope to "...rescue here a soul and there a household, now an infant and again a dying adult." One year later he told Madame Aulneau that God had made use of him, and that through his efforts, an entire Native family was received into the faith. "My main occupation this last winter was to instruct the father of this family,"[108] he wrote, describing how the members of the family received the sacraments of baptism, marriage, and Eucharist. His main concern was the reprehensible conduct of the French in the area, who created a stumbling block in spreading the Gospel. He was also worried about the Native's malnourishment, a result of their wandering lifestyle. Father DuJaunay was truly devoted to the Ottawa, and was happy when, in 1741, he was able to teach their language to Father de La Morinie.[109] The conditions at Michilimackinac were hardly favorable to uninterrupted Native American ministry, and he requested to be transferred to work among the Mandans, a more sedentary people to the west.[110] His request was never granted, but great changes occurred at Michilimackinac due to his ministerial efforts.

The reconstructed 1743 Ste. Anne's Church at Michilimackinac.
(Photo credit: *Mackinac State Historic Parks*)

The early 1740's was a period of

Photo of Ste. Anne medallion found by archaeologists at Michilimachinac. (Photo credit: *Mackinac State Historic Parks*)

immense development in the Catholic community in the Straits area. The local church structure, which was in a dilapidated condition, was razed and a new impressive building was constructed in 1743 under the direction of master carpenter Joseph Ainse. This church was built to serve the French residents of Michilimackinac, and was dedicated to Ste. Anne. Ste. Anne, piously believed to be the grandmother of Christ, was held in high regard among all French Canadians, but especially among the *voyageurs*. To the local Ottawa tribe, which had now moved about 20 miles west to *L'Arbre Croche*, went the original mission of St. Ignace. Moreover, to alleviate the Native's beleaguered condition, a farm was established and run by Brother Jean-Baptiste-Nicolas Demers, S.J. The Jesuits would split their time between the two missions, and to help in the task, Father DuJaunay was also assisted by two new arrivals: Fathers de La Morinie and Coquart.

The arrival of Brother Demers, who was at times referred to as "Ruffert,"[111] was another turning point in the mission's history. His presence marks the first time that the Jesuits attempted self-sufficiency by the use of their own labor, and the first time that the mission was truly in a position to help others with its own surplus. Jean-Baptiste-Nicolas Demers was born on the 12th of January 1722, at Saint-Nicolas near Quebec. He was thus one of the few Jesuits to be born in the New World. He joined the Society of Jesus in 1748 at Quebec, and was assigned to the Mackinac mission while still a novice. His presence there marked the first time that Jesuit training was actually conducted at Mackinac. Other priests had made their final vows at this remote mission station, but Brother Demers was the first and only Jesuit to ever make his *first* vows at Michilimackinac. The

Cahier des vœux in the Jesuit archives of Montreal records the fact that during mass, Brother Demers pronounced the following formula before the consecrated Eucharist:

> Almighty and eternal God, I, Jean-Baptiste-Nicolas Demers, though altogether most unworthy in Your divine sight, yet relying on Your infinite goodness and mercy and moved with a desire of serving You, in the presence of the most Holy Virgin Mary and Your whole heavenly court, vow to Your Divine Majesty perpetual poverty, chastity, and obedience in the Society of Jesus; and I promise that I shall enter that same Society in order to lead my entire life in it, understanding all things according to its Constitutions. Therefore I suppliantly beg Your Immense Goodness and Clemency, through the blood of Jesus Christ, to deign to receive this holocaust in an odor of sweetness; and that just as You gave me the grace to desire and offer this, so You will also bestow abundant grace to fulfill it. Michilimackinac, Ste. Anne's Church, the Province of New France, 16th of July, 1750.[112]

Father DuJaunay received the vows, and Father Gabriel Marcol entered them in the official Jesuit records. Upon pronouncing these vows, Jean-Baptiste Demers became an approved *Temporal Coadjutor* in the Society of Jesus. Brother Demers was a great asset to the running of the mission, and is listed in the Jesuit directories of the time as "administrator of all offices."[113]

The new arrangement of the missions worked well and facilitated greater care to both the Ottawa and the French. While working with souls at L'Arbre Croche, Father DuJaunay also occupied himself with the compilation of a French-Ottawa dictionary. This massive volume numbers 851 pages and is filled with dedications to pious individuals. The protection of a holy patron is implored at the beginning of each new letter. For example, entries found with the letter "A" are placed under the protection of the Assumption of Mary, with "B" entries the dictionary recognizes the Immaculate Conception, for "E" entries the intercession of Saint Joseph is referenced, and so forth.[114] Father DuJaunay eloquently ended his work with the following conclusion:

> O God, I built a monument more fragile than glass and lighter than flying with a feather and flax, which, without Your care, either the devouring rain or the consuming force of the flame, in a short time will consume. O you who read these words, put them right, correct them, for indeed in Barbaria there are many barbarities to banish, a new language for the stammerers you devise, and wondrously, a few jewels of the crown for those watching.
> This work such as it is, was just now completed on 7 June 1748. When, at some certain time, the Michilimackina glade may be allayed, the sound of the insults to us will be of the woodland threats.[115]

Clearly Father DuJaunay was a dedicated pastor, and he was heartbroken when, in the wake of the 1757 smallpox epidemic, he returned to

Michilimackinac from a visit in Montreal, and found a devastated community. Only Father Marin-Louis Le Franc was present to perform the necessary funerals and sacraments. In 1758, Father DuJaunay wrote to Monsieur Langlade and informed him that the farm at L'Arbre Croche would be unable to supply him with any corn. Of the conditions, Father DuJaunay wrote, "This is a year of crisis and desolation for those of us from Michilimackinac."[116] Other tragedies befell both the French and Native people, but none brought about as much change as the Seven Years' War.

The 600-year old rivalry between the French and English Monarchies was also played out in each nation's respective American claims. From 1756 until 1763, the Seven Years War raged in Europe between England and France, and the North American theater of this conflict is generally called the French and Indian War. Bolstered by their Native American allies, the French held the upper hand at the start, but the tide soon turned when the British renewed their efforts under Prime Minister William Pitt. The most decisive battle occurred in 1759, on the Plains of Abraham near Quebec, where General James Wolfe defeated the Marquis de Montcalm. As a result, the British soon gained control of Canada. The French posts in the Great Lakes were turned over to the British, yet in many ways, life remained the same. The British were tolerant in their treatment of the French, and allowed the practice of Roman Catholicism to continue. At Michilimackinac the transition seemed uneventful at first, and both Natives and Frenchmen appear to have accepted the new leadership. In May of 1761, while waiting for the arrival of the British flag, Father DuJaunay wrote the following to his superior, Father Jean-Baptiste de Saint-Pé:

> We are at present here, all three [Fathers DuJaunay and LeFranc, and Brother Demers]. Father *LeGrave* [LeFranc] is to return tomorrow to the fort, where we are waiting from day to day the English from Detroit. There is some opposition, but only on the part of some *Saulteurs* [Chippewas]. We keep a pretty tight reign on those who are within our reach, but we fear some trouble is on the way. What I can assure you of, from certain knowledge, is that neither Monsieur Langlade nor any other Frenchman has any intention except the obedience due to that which has been arranged between the two generals. Our needs are too great for us to dispense with the presence, or at least the assistance, of our conquerors. It is only this spring that these sparks have burst forth; all winter everything has been very tranquil around us, and I learn that the Ottawa chiefs from Grand River, who have not yet arrived, have nothing but peaceful notions.[117]

As for the Jesuits' reaction to the transition, Father DuJaunay reported that Brother Demers had fed three Englishmen who had wintered at the fort. The hunger was so rampant among those returning from the west, that the abundant harvest would scarcely carry them through the season. The following year Father Saint-Pé wrote to Father DuJaunay to inform him that while the Jesuits had been kicked out of the college in Quebec and that there was much work to be done, all was (for the most part) in working condition. Father Coquart was back on mission, Father de La Morinie was among the Illinois, and Father Potier had returned to Detroit after a year's absence.[118]

While the British may have been wise in their dealings with the French, they were less so in their relations with the Native Americans. The British had little tolerance for the French practice of gift-giving, and even less interest in continuing the French practice of donating ammunition, food, and other items to the tribes. The British triumph thus brought confusion and anger among the tribes, which escalated into war. In the spring of 1763, an Ottawa chief by the name of Pontiac spearheaded a campaign. Though ultimately unsuccessful, the uprising achieved some dramatic victories and made it clear that the Natives were a force to be reckoned with. At Michilimackinac, the Native forces were lead by Chief Minavavana, or as the French called him, *Le Grand Saulteur*. This chief had sworn that he would ever remain the avowed enemy of the possessors of Michilimackinac, and that the territory on which the fort was built belonged to him. To the English traveller Jonathan Carver, who learned of his views, Chief Minavavana said, *"Cawin nishishin saganosh"*; that is, "The English are no good."[119]

Minavavana organized the Natives' plans for the attack on the British garrison. On June 4th, 1763, under the pretense of playing a game of

Reconstructed Priest's House at Michilimackinac. Here Father DuJaunay protected British traders during the 1763 Indian attack. (Photo credit: *Mackinac State Historic Parks*)

Lacrosse, the Natives gained entrance into the fort and massacred most of the English occupants. Of the Jesuits' role on that fatal day, Father François Philibert Watrin, S.J. wrote on the 3rd of September 1764:

> [The Natives] had already destroyed a large part of [the fort] when Father DuJaunay, a Jesuit, opened his house to serve as an asylum to what remained of the soldiers and of the English traders; but to save their life, he greatly endangered his own. The savage youth, irritated at seeing half of their prey snatched away from them, tried to make amends for their loss at the expense of Father DuJaunay; and the old men of the nation had difficulty in pacifying them.[120]

Following the attack, Michilimackinac was in chaos. The Natives broke into the liquor supply, and those Englishmen who were not killed were badly abused. Captain George Etherington turned the command of the post over to Charles Langlade, and both solicited Father DuJaunay's assistance. Father DuJaunay discouraged an effort to retake possession of the fort, stating that the results could be even more disastrous.[121] Instead, he would use his high standing among the Ottawa to go on a peacekeeping mission to Detroit. On June 12th, 1763, Father DuJaunay and fifteen Natives left Michilimackinac bearing a letter for Major Gladwyn of Detroit. In the letter Captain Etherington recounted the events that had taken place, requested supplies, and made tentative plans for the future. In the context of the letter, Etherington states:

> I have been very much obliged to... the Jesuit for the many good offices [he] has done us on this occasion. The Priest seems inclinable to go down to your post for a day or two, which I am very glad of, as he is a very good man, and had a great deal to say with the savages, hereabout, who will believe everything he tells them, on his return, which I hope will be soon. ...I refer you to the Priest for the particulars of this melancholy affair...[122]

Father DuJaunay and his company made good time, and they arrived in Detroit on June 18th, where he stayed with Father Potier. Two days later, on Father DuJaunay's initiative, a council was held with Pontiac concerning the liberty of the English.[123] His duties faithfully fulfilled, Father DuJaunay met with Major Gladwyn and departed for Michilimackinac with the required information. Of the meeting, an observer wrote:

> This morning the commanding officer gave the Jesuit some memorandum of what he should say to the Indians and French at Michilimackinac, as also to Captain Etherington, as he did not choose to carry a letter saying that if he was asked by the Indians if he had any he would be obliged to say yes, as he never told a lie in his life. He gave him a belt to give to the Ottawas there, desiring him to tell them that he was very well pleased with their not meddling in an affair that must end in their ruin.

That if they send their prisoners to Montreal, it will convince the General of their Intentions for which they will be probably well rewarded.

[He was] to give his compliments to Misters Langlade and Farli and thank them for their good offices which he exhorts them to continue. To desire them to try and prevent as much as possible all commerce with our enemies, above all ammunition and arms. That he authorizes Mr. Langlade to command in the fort according to the orders given him by Captain Etherington till further orders.[124]

Upon his return from Detroit, Father DuJaunay continued to work for peace among the Natives. In August of 1763, the Ottawa elders met at his house and attempted to bring about some tranquility. Drunkenness followed, however, and at one point Brother Demers was struck by an intoxicated Ottawa and made to bleed. Eventually the Natives regained Father DuJaunay's confidence, and the following summer he was able to vouch for their right conduct to the British official, Sir William Johnson. During a Calumet ceremony of peace with Sir Johnson, the Ottawas of L'Arbre Croche presented a letter from Father DuJaunay, "containing strong assurances of their good behavior."[125]

The British domination of Canada, as well as internal conflicts in France and within the Roman Catholic Church, adversely affected Jesuit missions. Father DuJaunay was recalled to Quebec as a result of this situation, and there was little hope for a successor. The fact that he took the church's sacred vessels with him to Detroit[126] indicates the gravity of the situation. Father DuJaunay spent his last years with the Ursuline sisters, and at age 76 he died "...full of virtue and good works."[127] The era of the Mackinac Jesuits had come to an end.

Chapter Six: "...they regret his loss as if it was the first day."

-Father Pierre Gibault, in referring to the Ottawa of Pierre DuJaunay, S.J. 1768

The Jesuit missions in the Great Lakes were all officially closed around the year 1765, but this event was long in coming. In Europe, as well as in the worldwide colonies, the Society of Jesus had managed to make many political and ecclesiastical enemies. The Jesuit Reductions in Paraguay met with opposition due to their economic success, and for their provision of sanctuary for Natives who would otherwise have been profitable slaves. Religious leaders were opposed to what they considered pagan practices (eg. Chinese Rites Controversy) in the Jesuit missions, and they accused the Society of Jesus of moral laxity. In time, Jesuits were expelled from country after country, and eventually, in 1773, Pope Clement XIV suppressed the entire order. As Canada was then under Protestant England, edicts from Rome could be neglected, and the Society of Jesus died a slow death. At Mackinac there were some people who remembered the Jesuits up until 1825.

The first and greatest hostility towards the Society of Jesus occurred in Portugal, in the person of Don Sebastian Carvalho, the Marquis de Pombal. Upon taking the office of prime minister, he severely restricted the Jesuits' work, and following an assassination attempt on King Joseph I, he blamed the Society of Jesus. In January of 1759, Jesuit property was confiscated, and the following September, all Jesuits were expelled from the kingdom.

In France similar events occurred. The Jesuits' controversies with the Jansenists created many enemies, and their ecclesiastical and political influence aroused jealousy among other religious orders. Louis XV was influenced by those surrounding him, and only the smallest excuse was needed to attack the order. This came when Father Antoine de Lavalette, S.J., the procurator-general of the Jesuit missions in the Caribbean Islands, incurred a tremendous debt to some merchants in Lyon. As Father de Lavalette could not pay the bill, the entire order was charged. In the ensuing trial, the Jesuits' constitutions were examined, and many of their publications were ordered to be burned by the public executioner. In 1761, against Louis XV's wishes, the Parliament of Paris closed all the Jesuit colleges in its jurisdiction. The following year, all Jesuit estates were confiscated and the order was suppressed in the province. Finally, a royal decree on December 1st, 1764 dissolved the Society of Jesus throughout the king's dominions. Comparable events took place in Spain and her colonies, as well as in many Italian states. In the summer of 1773, Pope Clement XIV issued the brief, *Dominus ac redemptor*, which abolished the order throughout the world.

England had allowed the practice of Catholicism to continue in Quebec, although the position of Catholics in the province was certainly delicate. When Bishop Jean-Olivier Briand received the news of suppression, he felt the circumstances called for discretion. The British government had already been embarrassed by the Quebec Act, which was interpreted in the English-speaking colonies as selling out to the Church of Rome, and Bishop Briand wanted no more trouble. Also, since the British takeover, it had already been decided to let the Jesuits die out, without molesting them. Thus the Bishop called together the remaining Jesuits and told them of their fate. Later he reported to Mesdames de Pontbriand that:

> Our Jesuits here still wear the Jesuit cassock, still have the reputation of Jesuits, carry out the duties of Jesuits, and in Canada it is only the governor, I and my secretary, who know they are no longer Jesuits, they excepted. I am giving a report to the sovereign pontiff of all my actions..., informing him that I have established the same superior and attorney who will manage the estates under my orders.[128]

The Jesuits attempted to stay together, and while Father DuJaunay resided with the Ursuline sisters, both he and Father Le Franc were attached to the Jesuit college. The last of the original French Jesuits to die was Father Jean-Joseph Casot, S.J., on March 16th, 1800.

The Catholic community at Michilimackinac, having suffered a great

Colonial Michilimackinac in Mackinaw City has been reconstructed by the Mackinac State Historic Parks to its appearance of the 1770s. (Photo credit: *Mackinac State Historic Parks*)

loss with the departure of Father DuJaunay, longed for a replacement. Father Pierre Gibault, a priest of the Paris Foreign Mission Society, was an occasional visitor to Ste. Anne's Parish, but was no substitute for a permanent pastor. Three years into Father DuJaunay's absence, Father Gibault spent a few days at Michilimackinac and wrote to Bishop Briand:

> ...On arriving at this post, after dining with the commander, I went to the confessional which I did not leave for ten hours and this is the only day I have left it early. I also had some baptisms to perform but only one marriage ceremony. I have had some distress and sorrow in my short sojourn here, but also some consolation. My distress arose from being unable to remain long enough to respond to the eagerness of the great number of *voyageurs* who asked me to hear their confessions. Some have not been to confession for from three to ten years. ...In a word, God has not been wholly forgotten by these people. ...I have been visited here by the savages of Father DuJaunay; they regret his loss as if it was the first day. Those who speak French have come to confession; others wished to, but we could not understand each other.[129]

Father DuJaunay's former flock hungered for spiritual leadership. Meanwhile, the parish of Ste. Anne's continued under lay leadership, and the farm at L'Arbre Croche remained in operation. In 1799 Father Gabriel Richard, S.S., a French Sulpician, visited the Straits region and was quite distressed over the spiritual state of affairs. He reported to Bishop John Carroll that while a recently deceased chief had been baptized, the Catholic faith was almost lost among the remaining 1,300 inhabitants. Father Richard found the Natives "more attached to strong liquor than to any religious practices."[130]

When Henry R. Schoolcraft, the American Indian agent, passed through the Straits in September of 1820, he noted that the Ottawa farm was producing enough food for their own consumption, as well as a surplus to offer at the Michilimackinac market. The site of the former chapel and Jesuit residence was pointed out to him by his guides, who called it *Pointe à la Mission*.[131] A similar observation was made in 1822 by Jedediah Morse, who was making a report on Indian affairs to the Secretary of War. He felt that the "improved state and appearance" of the Natives was the fruit of the Jesuits' labors.[132] Yet, the Natives' material affairs were not the full scope of their concern, and they went to great means to try and obtain another Jesuit. In 1823 members of the Ottawa nation from L'Arbre Croche sent President James Monroe and the United States Congress the following petition:

> We the undersigned, Chiefs, heads of families and others of the Tribe of the Ottawas residing at Waganakisi (the Arbre Croche, i.e., Crooked Tree) on the lower eastern shore of Lake Michigan, take this mode to communicate

our wants and wishes to our most respected Father, the President of the U. S. We return our best thanks to our Father and to Congress for his and their exertions to bring us, your very affectionate children, to civilization and to the knowledge of JESOUS, the Redeemer of the red skins as well as of the white people.

Trusting on your paternal affection, we come forward, and claiming liberty of conscience, we most earnestly pray, that you may be pleased to let us have a teacher or a minister of the Gospel belonging to the same Denomination of Christians to which did belong the members of the Catholic missionary Society of St. Ignatius established at Michilimakinac, or at the Arbre Croche, by F[ather] Marquet and others of the Order of the Jesuits. During a great many years they have resided amongst us, occupied and cultivated a field on our own ground, and instructed our fathers in the first principles of Christianity and agriculture.

Such teachers we have long since wished and continue to wish to have. Such teachers, appointed by your paternal affection, we invite to come and settle on the same spot occupied, until the year 1765, by F[ather] Dujaunay, that is to say, on the shore of Lake Michigan, near the lower end of our village at the Arbre Croche.

For so doing and granting to us, your devoted children, this their humble petition, we will forever feel very grateful and will pray the Great Spirit to bless you and your white children. In witness whereof we have made our *tautems* (marks) on this day, the 12th of August, A.D., 1823.

Alexandre Baurassa, John D. Losly. Thémains; (witnesses)

Macate Binessi (Black-Bird), the main chief at Arbre Croche; Pakosigane (Gull), the first chief at Arbre Croche; Jaguaganai (Crane); Walogogue (Black-Bass); Inssagon (Bear); Okigurivanon (Fish); Chawano (Spit); Giwentarido (Fish); Seginicana (Spit); Gadabasache (Hare); Nisbinici (Eel); Gochanae (Bear); Ochachibecodo (Stag); Michiani (Falcon); Chasnigoin (Bear); Kakychicohone (Eagle); Mideois (Fish); Tondagoni (Bear-Foot); Omascos (Elk); Nakanaci (Duck); Pesacige (Eagle); Wakechimant (Fish); Kinochameg (Deer); Ogisthigami (Fish); Pidobig (Eagle); Nakanikaso (Partridge); Neskezi (Deer); Pakosch (Falcon); Sabanimiki (Fish-Hawk); Ciwetagan (Trout).

W. McGulpin

Matthew McGulpin.[133]

While the request did not bring forth a Jesuit, 1823 saw the arrival of the first Protestant institutions. Reverend William M. Ferry, a Presbyterian minister, opened the "Mission School" on Mackinac Island, where he educated Native American children and found favor with the new American social class. Father Jean Dejean, a French secular priest, served the Native population from 1827-30, but the request for a Jesuit in the area was not granted until 1846, and then by way of Canada. The last known remembrance of the Mackinac Jesuits came in 1825, when Father Francis Vincent Badin visited L'Arbre Croche. An elderly Christian Ottawa, "pointed out the place where the 'black robe' used to walk up and down while reading his breviary."[134]

Epilogue:

In the long tradition of the worldwide Society of Jesus, the Jesuits at Mackinac played an important role in shaping the area's history. Fathers Claude Dablon and Jacques Marquette began the mission of St. Ignace with a small band of Native American Christians, who were seeking safer grounds. Yet that was only the beginning, and as the young mission grew, so did the European population. Fathers Philippe Pierson and Henri Nouvel helped to facilitate in this difficult transition. Conflicts with political and military personnel, most notably Antoine de la Mothe Cadillac, lead to bitter disagreements and the temporary closure of the mission by Fathers Étienne de Carheil and Joseph-Jacques Marest. A new era began on the Southern shore of the Straits of Mackinac, and was dominated by Father Pierre DuJaunay's dual Native and European Christian congregations, as well as Brother Jean-Baptiste-Nicolas Demer's mission farm. The basic focus of the Jesuits' ministry was the religious and physical development of Native American communities. Apart from this, interaction with Europeans existed from the time Father Marquette first charted the Mississippi River, to when Father DuJaunay helped establish peace with the British following Pontiac's Uprising. The Jesuit presence at the Straits of Mackinac continued until 1765, when political and religious

Ste. Anne's Church at Colonial Michilimackinac (Photo credit: *Mackinac State Historic Parks*)

developments far from this wilderness post forced the closure of the mission.

The end may have come, but few ideas and dreams, if any, die out completely. In Europe, Empress Catherine the Great of Russia refused to allow the Decree of Suppression to be promulgated in her empire. As a result, the Jesuits in Russia continued administering their schools. At the same time, Jesuits in the American Colonies continued to work under the name of "The Catholic Gentlemen of Maryland," and the leadership of John Carroll, a former Jesuit who became the first bishop in the United States.

Forty-one years after *Dominus ac redemptor*, in a world forever changed by the French Revolution, Rome entered a period of greater ecclesiastic stability and the time seemed right to restore the Jesuits to sure standing. Pope Pius VII accomplished this task on August 7th, 1814. After celebrating mass at the altar of St. Ignatius in the Church of the Gesù, Rome, he published the bull *Sollicitudo Omnium* reinstating the Society of Jesus throughout the world. The first Jesuits returned to Canada in 1842, and they soon began to trace their old footprints.

Father DuJaunay had performed his last baptism at Mackinac on July 3rd, 1765, and one day shy of 81 years later, Father Pierre Point, S.J., performed the same sacrament on July 2nd, 1846, at Sault Ste. Marie.[135] Except for a brief period during the 1860's, Jesuits staffed St. Mary's Parish from 1846 until 1914, when they sought to move more into Native American ministry. The best-known of this later group of missionaries was Father William Gagnieur, S.J., who traveled throughout the Eastern Upper Peninsula from 1892 until his death in 1937. While his main ministry was to the Chippewa, Father Gagnieur was also known in lumber camps, convents, and shipyards. In my younger days, I remember my grandparents and their friends speaking of this saintly man. Supposedly his hardness of hearing made confession difficult, and at times embarrassing. One woman told me of a time when the snow had stranded her in Hessel, and she slept under his bearskin rug! Father Gagnieur was followed by Father Paul Prud'homme, S.J., who made his way from Paris, to Sault Ste. Marie, Ontario, to St. Ignace, where he took up residence with the Ursuline sisters. From his base in St. Ignace, Father Prud'homme was the traveling priest for over twenty-five different locations. When he was in St.Ignace, my father served as an acolyte of his mass. During this time of technological advancement, the Upper Peninsula began to catch up with the rest of the world, and Father Prud'homme questioned the need for his services. In

1956, he wrote a letter to his superior in which he stated:

> Being always in contact with white people and easy living conditions, it is difficult to keep our missionary and religious spirit; I imagine that the inevitable hardships that the missionaries meet in India, China or elsewhere, help them to keep that spirit alive. Here it is easy to get away from hardships. Making contact, meeting nice people, spending hours in their homes, trying to get more and more money is not important. It does not help to develop the missionary spirit and to be more regular in our duties of our religious life. ...If we are too anxious to have everything comfortable in the missions: electric blankets, electric sheets, comfortable bedding and heating, something has been lacking in the missionary preparation.[136]

Perhaps it was not because of the evil inherent in electric sheets, but in the fall of 1959, Father John McGrail, S.J., the Provincial of the Detroit Province Society of Jesus, closed the majority of the Native American mission stations. The parish of St. Isaac Jogues remained under Jesuit administration, and Father Joseph Lawless, S.J., continued to visit various missions, but by car rather than by snowshoe or canoe.

When I was a student at Lake Superior State College, I once rode my bike past St. Isaac Jogues Parish and encountered Father Bernard Haas, S.J. Three days later I met with the Provincial, Father Howard Gray, S.J., and asked if I might join the Jesuits. Father Thomas Bain, S.J. helped in the decision of my entrance into the order. Our Jesuit commitment to the Diocese of Marquette lasted until 1992, when, despite my pleas, the new Provincial, Father Joseph Daoust, S.J., ended our presence there. It was Father Daoust's conviction that there was no longer anything distinctly Jesuit needed at the parish. Around the same time he committed our apostolic efforts to an inner city parish in Columbus, Ohio, and began preparations to open a new high school, Loyola Academy, in Detroit. Both works minister to populations in great need, and, while I might not personally approve of the change, I feel confident that St. Ignatius of Loyola, Father Marquette, and Brother Demers would.

It has already been proven with the suppression in 1773 and, for that matter, during the fifteen centuries which preceded the efforts of Ignatius of Loyola, that the Catholic Church might not be as interesting without Jesuits, but it hardly needs them for survival. In the case of Sault Ste. Marie, St. Ignace, Mackinaw City, and Mackinac Island, the church, absent the Jesuits, thrives. In St. Ignace one can still see the grave of Father Marquette, or visit his national memorial. The local parish, named in honor of St. Ignatius Loyola, dates to the time of the first Bishop of the Diocese of Marquette, Frederick Baraga. Mackinaw City, aside from its log reconstruction of Ste. Anne's at Colonial Michilimackinac, is also home to St. Anthony's Parish. The original faith community served by Father DuJaunay continues in the form of Ste. Anne's on Mackinac Island. If one opens the parish register his handwriting can still be seen. The penmanship is terrible.

For more information on how you can be a part of the ministries of the Detroit Province Society of Jesus, or the Diocese of Marquette, write to:

Detroit Province Society of Jesus
7303 W. Seven Mile Rd.
Detroit, Mi. 48221-2198

Diocese of Marquette
Post Office Box 550
Marquette, Mi. 49855

NOTES

Author's Preface

[1] 1. Ignatius of Loyola, *The Constitutions of the Society of Jesus* (St. Louis: The Institute of Jesuit Sources, 1970) edited by George Ganss, S.J. #152, 216.

Chapter One

[2] 1. In a letter of 1541 to Fathers Salmeron and Broet, Ignatius wrote: " Whenever we wish to win someone over and engage him in the greater service of God our Lord, we should use the same strategy for good which the enemy employs to draw a good soul to evil. **He enters through the other's door and comes out his own.** He enters with the other by not opposing his ways but by praising them. He acts familiarly with the soul, suggesting good and holy thoughts which bring peace to the good soul. Later he tries, little by little, to come out his own door, always suggesting some error or illusion under the appearance of good, but which will always be evil. So we with a good purpose can praise or agree with another concerning some particular good thing, dissembling whatever else may be wrong. After thus gaining his confidence, we shall have better success. In this sense we go in with him his way but come out our own." Ignatius of Loyola, *Letters of St.Ignatius of Loyola* (Chicago: Loyola University Press, 1959)edited by William Young, S.J., pp. 51-52.

[3] 2. Archives Nationales, Colonies (Paris, n.d.), serie C11 B, vol. I, pp. 427-428. Hereafter cited as ANP.

[4] 3. Reuben G. Thwaites, ed., *The Jesuit Relations and Allied Documents* (New York: Pageant Book Co., 1959), vol. L p. 173. This work is hereafter cited as JR.

[5] 4. André Letendre, *La grande aventure des Jésuites au Québec* (Beauport, Québec: Impressions J.L. Inc., 1991), p. 55.

[6] 5. ANP Colonies serie C11 A, vol 58 pp. 71-72.

[7] 6. F.B. Dexter, "Estimates of population in the American colonies," *Proceedings of the American Antiquarian Society* (Worcester, Mass: American Antiquarian Society, 1887), vol. V p.50.

[8] 7. Jean-Baptiste Ferland, *La France dans l'Amérique du Nord* (Montréal: Granger Frères Limitée, 1865), vol. III, pp. 341-2. Citing "Le recensement fait par M. de Beauharnois en 1744."

[9] 8. G.B. Nash,"The Image of the Indian in the Southern Colonial Mind," Dudley and Novak, eds., *Wild Man Within* (Pittsburgh: University of Pittsburgh Press, 1972), p.72.

[10] 9. Ralph Hamor, *A True Discourse of the Present Estate of Virginia,* (London: John Beale, 1615), p. 36.

[11] 10. Brian Fagan, *Clash of Cultures* (New York: W.H. Freeman and Company, 1984), p. 199.

[12] 11. Fagan, *Cultures*, p.199.

[13] 12. François De Laval *Mandement pour Excommunier ceux qui vendent des Boissons Enivrantes aux Sauvages*, May 5, 1660. Gagnon and Têtu, eds., *Mandements, lettres pastorales et circulaires des évêques de Québec* (Québec: Imprimerie Générale A. Coté et Cie, 1887), vol. I, pp. 14-15. See also pp. 30, 42, 43.

[14] 13. JR vol. V, p. 251.

[15] 14. JR vol. LIV, pp. 134-136.

[16] 15. The Natives of Reverend Eliot's "praying" towns, started in 1651, were forbidden from idleness, adultery, physical abuse, or shifting their wigwams. Hairstyles were controlled along with clothing, and one was not to "kill their lice betweene their teeth."[sic] If the rules were broken one could be fined up to twenty shillings or be beat. John Eliot, "The Day-breaking, if Not the Sun-rising of the Gospel" as reprinted in Washburn, Wilcomb, eds. *The Indian and the White Man* (Garden City, New York: Doubleday and Company, Inc., 1964) p. 186.

[17] 16. JR vol. XII, p. 117.

[18]17. JR vol. LV, p.115.

Chapter Two

[19]1. JR vol.LV, pp. 157-159.

[20]2. Gilbert Garraghan, "Some Hitherto Unpublished Marquettiana," *Mid-America* vol.18, new series, vol.7, no.1, January 1936, p.15. Garraghan explains that the normal course of philosophy at Pont-à-Mousson lasted three years. The second year, in which Marquette was enrolled, was devoted mostly to the natural sciences and went by the name of "physics."

[21]3. Garraghan, "Marquettiana," p. 16.

[22]4. Emma Blair, ed., *The Indian Tribes of the Upper Mississippi Valley and the Region of the Great Lakes* (Cleveland: The Arthur H. Clark Co., 1911) vol. I p.336.

[23]5. JR vol. LIV, p.177.

[24]6. Nicolas Perrot, *Memoire sur les moeurs, coustumes et religion des sauvages de l'Amerique Septrionale* (Leipzig, 1864) p. 99. See also JR vol. LVI, p. 115.

[25]7. Pierre Chaumonot, S.J., *Autobiographie et pièces Inédites* (Paris: Oudin, 1869) p.52. Edited by Auguste Carayon, translation by J. Boynton.

[26]8. JR vol. XLIV, p.175-81 tells of Father Dablon's escape from death, and vol. XXIII recounts his travels up the Saguenay.

[27]9. JR vol. LV, p. 161.

[28]10. Each year a Jesuit is to make a renewal of the *Spiritual Exercises* in an eight-day silent retreat. This practice was instituted with Decree 29 of General Congregation VI under Father General Aquaviva in 1608, and is often referred to in the correspondence of the Mackinac Jesuits. Usually this was carried out in conjunction with other Jesuits at a mission hub such as Sault Ste. Marie or Detroit. See *Institutum Societatis Iesu*, (Florentiae: 1893) vol. II, pp. 302-303.

First vows of poverty, chastity, and obedience are taken by a Jesuit after two years of novitiate and bind the man to the order for life. Final vows bring formal closure to a Jesuit's formation and signify that a man is fully accepted by the Society of Jesus. In the case of some of the Fathers, a fourth solemn vow of obedience to the Pope, in regards to mission, is also taken. As the mission at Michilimackinac increased in importance, these ceremonies would take place locally.

[29]11. JR vol. LVI pp. 117-119.

[30]12. JR vol. LVII p. 249.

[31]13. JR vol. LVII p. 251.

[32]14. JR vol. LVII p. 255.

[33]15. JR vol. LVII p. 259.

[34]16. JR vol. LVII p. 259.

[35]17. JR vol. LIX p. 91.

[36]18. Tonsure was the ceremony in which a portion of the hair was clipped or shaved, and signified the entrance to the clerical state. Ignatius had received tonsure even before his conversion.

[37]19. JR vol. LIX p. 91.

[38]20. The explorers went far enough to safely conclude that the Mississippi emptied into the Gulf of Mexico, but then they retreated for fear of encountering the Spanish. Upon return, Jolliet's canoe capsized and all of his records were lost. Marquette's map has survived and is preserved in *Les Archives de la Société de Jésus, Canada Français* at St.Jérôme, Québec, hereafter cited as ASJCF. The first French exploration to reach the Gulf via the Mississippi was headed by LaSalle some years later.

[39]21. Marquette's sound health and robust body are referred to in the letter from Father LeMercier to Father General Oliva, of September 1, 1668. This reference negates the notion that he had always been of delicate health. See Garraghan, p. 22. Marquette's illness started during the summer of 1674, and returned twice more before taking his life in May of 1675.

[40]22. JR vol. LIX, pp. 203-4.

[41]23. JR vol., LIX, pp. 207.

Chapter Three
[42]1. St. Francis Borgia was born on October 28, 1510, and was duke of Gandia, Spain. After the death of his wife he joined the Society of Jesus, and eventually became the third Father General, in the line of Ignatius Loyola. During Borgia's time, the Society's works in Florida and Peru were begun, and there was a great awareness of the mission effort. He also did much negotiation on behalf of Pope Pius V at the courts of Spain, Portugal, and France. As he was beatified in 1624, and canonized in 1671, he would have been the most recent saint of the order.

[43]2. JR vol. LX, pp. 209-211.

[44]3. JR vol. LXI, p. 11.

[45]4. JR vol. LXI, p. 105-107.

[46]5. Pope Benedict XIV formally ended the Chinese Rites controversy in 1742 with the constitution *Ex quo singulari*, and thus greatly hindered attempts to inculturate Christianity.

[47]6. JR vol. LXI, p. 109.

[48]7. JR vol. LXI, p. 121. This Christmas celebration, repeated in following years, was described as well by Father Thierry Beschefer, S.J. in the *Relation* of 1683. JR vol. LXII, pp. 195-197.

[49]8. JR vol. LXI, p. 125.

[50]9. JR vol. LXII, pp. 199-201. This method was often used by the Jesuits with great success. In 1683, Father Beschefer wrote to his superior in the above *Relation* that "this prediction of eclipses has always been one of the things that have most astonished our savages; and it has given them a higher opinion of their missionaries. This has gone so far that, when one of our fathers, some years ago, predicted to the Iroquois an eclipse, those barbarians desired the father to tell them the position of an army of their enemies, which as they had heard, was marching against them. 'Since thou knowest all that passes in the sky,' they said to him, 'thou canst not be ignorant of what passes on earth.'" Brother Guy Consolmagno, S.J., an astronomer of the Vatican Observatory, has confirmed that on April 10th, 1679, there was a 90% eclipse of the Sun at the Straits of Mackinac. The phenomenon started at 12:07p.m., peaked at 1:30p.m., and was over at 2:40p.m. Another eclipse occurred in January of 1683, but only 50% of the Sun was eclipsed on that day.

[51]10. JR vol. LXI, p. 123.

[52]11. JR vol. LXI, p. 131.

[53]12. JR vol. LXI, p. 131.

[54]13. Perrot, *Memoire*, p. 90.

[55]14. JR vol. LXI, p. 139.

[56]15. JR vol. LXI, p. 143-5. For a similar incident, in which a Native lad threw rocks at the church windows, thus occasioning councils and apologies, see JR vol. LXII, pp. 197-199.

[57]16. Cavelier de LaSalle, *Relation of the Discoveries and Voyages of Cavelier de La Salle from 1679 to 1681*, translated by Melville Anderson, (Chicago: The Caxton Club, 1901), pp. 38-39.

[58]17. Henri de Tonty, *Relation of Henri de Tonty Concerning the Explorations of LaSalle from 1678 to 1683*, translated by Melville Anderson, (Chicago: The Caxton Club, 1898), pp. 21-23.

[59]18. Louis Hennepin, *A New Discovery of a Vast Country in America*, edited and translated by Reuben G. Thwaites, (Chicago: A.C. McClurg & Co., 1903), vol. I, p. 312.

[60]19. Henri Joutel, *Joutel's Journal of La Salle's Last Voyage 1684-7*, edited and translated by Henry R. Stiles, (Albany, N.Y.: Joseph McDonough, 1906), p. 199.

[61]20. Joutel, *Journal*, p. 199.

[62]21. Baron de La Hontan, *Un outre-mer au xvii siècle*, edited by François de Nion, (Paris: Plon-Nourrit et Cie, 1900), pp. 180-181. Translation by J. Boynton.

Chapter Four

[63]1. Relation du Sieur de la Mothe Cadillac, Pierre Margry, ed., *Découvertes et établissements des français dans l'ouest et dans le sud de L'Amérique Septentrionale (1614-1754) Mémoires et Documents Originaux* (Paris: Imprimerie de D. Jouaust, 1883) vol. V, pp. 75-6 & 80. Translation by J. Boynton.

[64]2. Cadillac, 1695, as reprinted in Rev. J.A. Van Fleet, *Old and New Mackinac with Copious Extracts from Marquette, Hennepin, La Hontan, Alexander Henry and Others* (Grand Rapids, Mich: "The Lever" Book and Job Office, 1880) p. 27.

[65]3. Denonville to Minister, 12th June 1686, Margry vol. V, pp. 11-12.

[66]4. JR vol. LXV, p. 272.

[67]5. George Paré, *The Catholic Church in Detroit 1701-1888* (Detroit: The Gabriel Richard Press, 1951) p. 126, citing Margry, *Découvertes* V, ciii-iv.

[68]6. Carheil to Cadillac, 25th July, 1701, Margry, pp. 204-205.

[69]7. Cadillac to M. de la Touche, endorsed 31st August, 1703, *Michigan Pioneer and Historical Collections* (Lansing: Robert Smith Printing Co., State Printers and Binders, 1904) vol. XXXIII, p. 183. This collection will hereafter be referred to as MPHC.

[70]8. Joseph Marest to Cadillac, 28th July, 1701, MPHC vol. XXXIII, p. 103.

[71]9. JR vol. LXV, p. 191 & 195.

[72]10. Jean Mermet to Cadillac, 19th April, 1702, MPHC vol. XXXIII, p. 118.

[73]11. Joseph Marest to Cadillac, 30th May, 1702, MPHC vol. XXXIII, p. 121.

[74]12. Cadillac Papers, 25th March, 1708, MPHC vol. XXXIII, p. 383.

[75]13. Cadillac Papers, 25th September, 1702, MPHC vol. XXXIII, pp. 142 & 148.

[76]14. Joseph Marest to Cadillac, 12th May, 1703, MPHC vol. XXXIII, p. 160.

[77]15. Cadillac to Pontchartrain, 31st August, 1703, MPHC vol. XXXIII, p. 162.

[78]16. Cadillac Papers, 31st August, 1703, MPHC vol. XXXIII, p. 170.

[79]17. Cadillac Papers, 31st August, 1703, MPHC vol. XXXIII, p. 183.

[80]18. Mémoire du Roy [Louis XIV] au Sieur Marquis de Vaudreuil, Versailles, 9th June 1706, Margry vol. V, pp. 345-346.

[81]19. Cadillac Papers, 23rd July, 1708, MPHC vol. XXXIII, p. 388.

[82]20. Cadillac Papers, 23rd July, 1708, MPHC vol. XXXIII, p. 389.

[83]21. Cadillac Papers, 14th November, 1708, MPHC vol. XXXIII, pp. 450-451.

[84]22. Letter LII The post of Michillimakina and of the Outavois to Quebec, 1710, Camille de Rochemonteix, S.J., ed., *Relation par lettres de l'Amérique septentrionalle (années 1709 et 1710)* (Paris: Letouzey et Ané, Éditeurs, 1904) p. 131. Translation by J. Boynton. For a discussion of probable authorship see *Bulletin du Parler Français au Canada* October 1904 vol. III no. 2, and April 1905 vol. III no. 8.

[85]23. Father Joseph Marest to the Marquis de Vaudreuil, 21st June, 1712, MPHC vol. XXXIII, pp. 553 & 555.

[86]24. Father Joseph Marest to the Marquis de Vaudreuil, 6th July, 1712, MPHC vol. XXXIII. pp. 557-559.

[87]25. JR vol. LXVI, p. 281.

[88]26. JR vol. LXVI, pp. 283-285.

[89]27. St. Ignatius, *Constitutions*, # 540.

[90]28. P.F.X. de Charlevoix, *Journal d'un voyage fait par ordre du roi dans L'Amerique Septentrionnale* (Paris: Chez Nyon, Libraire, 1764) p. 279. Translation by J. Boynton.

[91]29. Letter II Father Sebastien Rasles to Monsieur His Brother, Nanrantsouak 12th October, 1723, William Ingraham Kip, ed., *The Early Jesuit Missions in North America* (New York: Wiley and Putnam, 1846) p. 32.

Chapter Five

[92]1. Examples of this can be seen in the *Catalogus Personarum et Officiorum Provinciæ Franciæ Societatis Jesu* (Exeunte Anno 1758 & 1759), pp. 36 both editions.

[93]2. Pierre Potier, S.J., 20th August, 1746, Robert Toupin, S.J., ed., *Les écrits de Pierre Potier: la culture savante en Nouvelle-France au XVIII siècle* (Ottawa: Les Presses de L'Université D'Ottawa, 1995) p. 324.

[94]3. Father Léonard Bonaventure, Récollet, to Father Pierre Potier, S.J., 5th August, 1746, Toupin, *Les écrits* pp. 612-613.

[95]4. Major De Peyster to Major Lernoult, Detroit, 31st July, 1781, Ernest J. Lajeunesse, C.S.B., ed., *The Windsor Border Region: Canada's Southernmost Frontier A Collection of Documents* (Toronto: University of Toronto Press, 1960) pp. 121- 123.

[96]5. Pierre DuJaunay to Mother Superior, O.S.U., 13th June, 1755, ASJCF 855-12. Translation by J. Boynton.

[97]6. Pierre DuJaunay to Mother Superior, O.S.U., 26th September, 1755, ASJCF 855-13.

[98]7. A *pall* is a linen chalice cover used in Roman Catholic liturgy.

[99]8. DuJaunay, ASJCF 855-13. Translation by J. Boynton.

[100]9. *Parish Register, Ste. Anne's Church*, (Mackinac Island, Michigan). The marriage and baptism records are reprinted in Reuben Gold Thwaites, ed., *Collections of the State Historical Society of Wisconsin* (Madison: Published by the Society, 1908 and 1910) vols. XVIII & XIX. This collection will hereafter be referred to as WHC (Wisconsin Historical Collections).

[101]10. Marcel Trudel *L'Eglise canadienne sous le régime militaire 1759-1764* (Québec: Les Presses Universitaires Laval, 1957), vol. II *les institutions*, p. 404.

[102]11. WHC vol. XVII, pp. 372-373.

[103]12. WHC vol. XVII, pp. 374-375.

[104]13. WHC vol. XVII, pp. 423-424.

[105]14. Pierre DuJaunay, 16th August, 1743, French Michilimackinac Translation Project (unpublished: Mackinac State Historic Parks).

[106]15. Joseph Tasse, "Memoir of Charles de Langlade," WHC vol. VII. pp. 127-128.

[107]16. Pierre DuJaunay to Madame Aulneau, 28th September, 1739, Arthur E. Jones, S.J., ed., *The Aulneau Collection 1734-1745* (Montreal: Archives of St. Mary's College, 1893) No. 29.

[108]17. Pierre DuJaunay to Madame Aulneau, 5th May, 1740, Jones, *The Collection*, No. 33.

[109]18. Pierre DuJaunay to Madame Aulneau, 25th May, 1741, Jones, *The Collection*, No. 38.

[110]19. Beauharnois to Maurepas, Quebec, 6th October, 1739, Lawrence J. Burpee, ed., *Journals and Letters of Pierre Gaultier de Varennes de La Vérendrye and His Sons* (Toronto: The Champlain Society, 1927) pp. 364-365.

[111]20. Pierre DuJaunay to Monsieur Langlade, 3rd August, 1763, WHC vol. VIII, p. 219.

[112]21. *Cahier des vœux*, 16th July, 1750, First vows of J.B. Demers, ASJCF. Other Jesuits who made their final vows at Michilimackinac include: Michel Guignas in 1718, Pierre-Luc DuJaunay in 1738, Jean-Baptiste de La Morinie in 1741, and Claude-Godefroy Coquart in 1742.

[113]22. *Catalogus* (1758 & 1759), p. 36 both editions.

[114]23. Father Pierre DuJaunay, *Dictionarium Gallico-8ata8ka* McGill University, McLennan Library, Bd (Ms) 281.

[115]24. DuJaunay, *Dictionarium* p. 851. Translation by Christopher Daignault, S.S.E.

[116]25. Father DuJaunay to Monsieur Langlade, 24th September, 1758, WHC vol. VIII p. 214.

[117]26. Father DuJaunay to Father Saint-Pé, Saint Ignace, 7th May, 1761, Public Records Office, London (Colonial Papers: America and West Indies: No. 96. Amherst to Pitt, 13th August, 1761, Annex No. 58). Translation by J. Boynton.

[118]27. Father Saint-Pé to Father DuJaunay, 16th February, 1762, Archives Françaises de la Compagnie de Jésus, G Bro 173-2.

[119]28. Jonathan Carver, *Travels Through America 1766-1768*, edited by Norman Gelb, (New York: John Wiley & Sons, Inc., 1993) p. 94.

[120]29. JR vol. LXX, pp. 251-253.

[121]30. Alexander Henry, *Travels & Adventures in Canada and the Indian Territories*

between the Years 1760 and 1776, edited by James Bain, (Boston: Little, Brown, & Company, 1901) p. 90.

[122]31. Geo. Etherington to Major Gladwyn, 12th June 1763, WHC vol. VII, pp. 162-163.

[123]32. Milo Milton Quaife, ed., *The Siege of Detroit in 1763: The Journal of Pontiac's Conspiracy and John Rutherfurd's Narrative of a Captivity* (Chicago: R.R. Donnelley & Sons Company, 1958), pp. 140-141 & 147.

[124]33. Franklin B. Hough, ed., *Diary of the Siege of Detroit in the War with Pontiac* (Albany, New York: J. Munsell, 1860) pp. 32-33.

[125]34. "An Indian Congress" and Sir William Johnson to Thomas Gage, 22nd August, 1764, Milton W. Hamilton ed., *The Papers of Sir William Johnson* (Albany: The University of the State of New York, 1953) vol. XI, pp. 273 & 336.

[126]35. Letter to Bishop Briand, 18th July, 1771, Archives de l'Archdiocèse de Québec, 7 CM 5. This letter explains, that at the time of writing, two chalices, two ciboria and two monstrances, which had been the property of the Michilimackinac mission, were in Detroit. It was hoped that someday they could be used there again.

[127]36. "Extrait textuel des annales des Ursulines de Québec," ASJCF 632 (5).

Chapter Six

[128]1. Bishop Briand to Mesdames de Pontbriand, quoted in Camille de Rochemonteix, S.J., *Les Jésuites et la Nouvelle-France au xviii siècle* (Paris: Alphonse Picard et Fils Èditeurs, 1906), vol. II, p. 214. Translation by J. Boynton.

[129]2. Father Gibault to Bishop Briand, 28th July, 1768, Joseph P. Donnelly, S.J., ed., *Pierre Gibault, Missionary 1737-1802* (Chicago: Loyola University Press, 1971), pp. 40-41.

[130]3. Father Gabriel Richard to Bishop John Carroll, November, 1799, M. N.-E. Dionne, *L'Abbé Gabriel Richard* (Québec: Imprimerie De S.-A. Demers, 1902), pp. 14-15. Translation by J. Boynton.

[131]4. Henry R. Schoolcraft, *Narrative Journal of Travels from Detroit Northwest Through the Great Chain of American Lakes to the Sources of the Mississippi River in the Year 1820* (Albany: E.&E. Hosford, 1821), pp. 402-403.

[132]5. Jedediah Morse, *A Report to the Secretary of War of the United States on Indian Affairs 1822* (St.Clair Shores, Mi.: Scholarly Press, Inc., 1972), p. 25.

[133]6. V.F. O'Daniel, O.P., *The Right Rev. Edward Dominic Fenwick, O.P* (New York: Frederick Pustet Co., 1920) pp. 300-02. Other copies of various similar documents are in existence; see also Paré, *Detroit*, p. 592.

[134]7. Richard R. Elliott, "Frederick Baraga Among the Ottawas" *The American Catholic Quarterly Review* vol. XXI, no. 81, January, 1896, p.108. Quoting the manuscripts of Rev. C. Verwyst, O.S.F., Indian missionary in Wisconsin.

Epilogue

[135]1. This fact is noted in a report given to the Detroit Province of the Society of Jesus by Father Paul Prud'homme, S.J. in January of 1949, Archives of the Detroit Province Society of Jesus. Rev. Antoine Ivan Rezek also states this in *A History of the Diocese of Sault Ste. Marie and Marquette* (Chicago: M.A. Donohue & Co., 1906) vol. I, p. 47. Documentation for this fact is complicated by the fact that the pages for July 1846 are missing from the Parish Register of St. Mary's Church, Sault Ste. Marie, Michigan.

[136]2. Father Prud'homme, S.J. to V.R. Leo D. Sullivan, S.J., 21st February, 1956, Archives of the Detroit Province Society of Jesus.

BIBLIOGRAPHY

MANUSCRIPT AND ARCHIVAL SOURCES

Archives de l'Archdiocèse de Québec
   7 CM 5

Archives Françaises de la Compagnie de Jésus, Paris
   G Bro 173-2

Archives of the Detroit Province Society of Jesus
   Province Letters, received from Paul Prud'homme, S.J.

Les Archives de la Société de Jésus, Canada Français, St. Jérôme, Québec
   632 (5)
   855-13
   855-12
   Cahier des vœux

Mackinac State Historic Parks, Lansing
   French Michilimackinac Translation Project
   16th, August, 1763

McGill University, McLennan Library, Montreal
   Bd (Ms) 281

Public Records Office, London
   Colonial Papers: America and West Indies: No. 96, Annex No. 58.

Ste. Anne's Church, Mackinac Island, Michigan
   Parish Register

St. Mary's Church, Sault Ste. Marie, Michigan
   Parish Register

PRINTED PRIMARY SOURCES

Archives Nationales, Colonies (Paris, n.d.), series C11 A, vol. 58 & C11 B, vol. 1.

Blair, Emma, ed., *The Indian Tribes of the Upper Mississippi Valley and the Region of the Great Lakes* (Cleveland: The Arthur H. Clark Co., 1911).

Burpee, Lawrence J., ed., *Journals and Letters of Pierre Gaultier de Varennes de La Vérendrye and His Sons* (Toronto: The Champlain Society, 1927).

Carver, Jonathan, *Travels Through America 1766-1768* (New York: John Wiley & Sons, Inc., 1993) edited by Norman Gelb.

Catalogus Personarum et Officiorum Provinciæ Franciæ Societatis Jesu (Exeunte Anno 1758 & 1759).

Charlevoix, P.F.X. de, *Journal d'un voyage fait par ordre du roi dans l'Amerique Septentrionnale* (Paris: Chez Nyon, Libraire, 1764).

Chaumonot, Pierre, *Autobiographie et pièces inédites* edited by Auguste Carayon, (Paris: Oudin, 1869).

Donnelly, Joseph, ed., *Pierre Gibault, Missionary 1737-1802* (Chicago: Loyola University Press, 1971).

Dudley & Novak, eds., *Wild Man Within* (Pittsburgh: University of Pittsburgh Press, 1972).

Gagnon and Têtu, eds., *Mandements, lettres pastorales et circulaires des évêques de Québec* (Québec: Imprimerie Générale A. Coté et Cie, 1887).

Garraghan, Gilbert, "Some Hitherto Unpublished Marquettiana" *Mid-America* vol. 18, new series, vol. 7, No. 1, January, 1936, pp. 15-26.

Hamilton, Milton W., ed., *The Papers of Sir William Johnson* (Albany: The University of the State of New York, 1953).

Hamor, Ralph, *A True Discourse of the Present Estate of Virginia* (London: John Beale, 1615).

Hennepin, Louis, *A New Discovery of a Vast Country in America* (Chicago: A.C. McClurg & Co., 1903), vol. I., edited and translated by Reuben G. Thwaites.

Henry, Alexander, *Travels & Adventures in Canada and the Indian Territories Between the Years 1760 and 1776* (Boston: Little, Brown, & Company, 1901) edited by James Bain.

Hough, Franklin B., ed., *Diary of the Siege of Detroit in the War with Pontiac* (Albany, N.Y.: J. Munsell, 1860).

Ignatius of Loyola, *Letters of St. Ignatius of Loyola* (Chicago: Loyola University Press, 1959) edited by William Young.

Ignatius of Loyola, *The Constitutions of the Society of Jesus* (St. Louis: The Institute of Jesuit Sources, 1970) edited by George Ganss, S.J.

Institutum Societatis Iesu (Florentiae: 1893) vol. II.

Jones, Arthur E., ed., *The Aulneau Collection 1734-1745* (Montreal: Archives of St. Mary's College, 1893).

Joutel, Henri, *Joutel's Journal of LaSalle's Last Voyage 1684-7* (Albany, N.Y.: Joseph McDonough, 1906) edited and translated by Henry R. Stiles.

Kip, William Ingraham, ed., *The Early Jesuit Missions in North America* (New York: Wiley and Putnam, 1846).

LaHontan, Baron de, *Un outre-mer au xvii siècle voyages au Canada du Baron de La Hontan* (Paris: Plon-Nourrit et Cie, 1900) edited by François de Nion.

Lajeunesse, Ernest, ed., *The Windsor Border Region: Canada's Southermost Frontier A Collection of Documents* (Toronto: University of Toronto Press, 1960).

LaSalle, Cavelier de, *Relation of the Discoveries and Voyages of Cavelier de La Salle from 1679 to 1681* (Chicago: The Caxton Club, 1898) translated by Melville Anderson.

Margry, Pierre, ed., *Découvertes et établissements des Français dans l'ouest et dans le sud de l'Amérique Septentrionale (1614-1754) mémoires et documents originaux* (Paris: Imprimerie de D. Jouaust, 1883). vol. V.

Michigan Pioneer and Historical Collections (Lansing: Robert Smith Printing Co., State Printers and Binders, 1904). vol. XXXIII.

Morse, Jedediah, *A Report to the Secretary of War of the United States on Indian Affairs 1822* (St.Clair Shores, Mi.: Scholarly Press, Inc., 1972).

Perrot, Nicolas, *Memoire sur les moeurs, coustumes et religion des sauvages de l'Amerique Septrionale* (Leipzig, 1864).

Quaife, Milo Milton, ed., *The Siege of Detroit in 1763: The Journal of Pontiac's Conspiracy and John Rutherfurd's Narrative of a Captivity* (Chicago: R.R. Donnelley & Sons Co., 1958).

Rochemonteix, Camille de, ed., *Relation par lettres de l'Amerique Septentrionalle (années 1709 et 1710)* (Paris: Letouzey et Ané, Éditeurs, 1904).

Schoolcraft, Henry R., *Narrative Journal of Travels from Detroit Northwest Through the Great Chain of American Lakes to the Sources of the Mississippi River in the Year 1820,* (Albany: E.&E.Hosford, 1821).

Thwaites, Reuben Gold, ed., *Collections of the State Historical Society of Wisconsin* (Madison: Published by the Society). vols. VIII (1879), XVII (1906), XIX (1910).

Thwaites, Reuben Gold, ed., *The Jesuit Relations and Allied Documents* (New York: Pageant Book Co., 1959). vols., V, XII, XLIV, L, LIV, LV, LVI, LVII, LIX, LX, LXI, LXII, LXV, LXVI, LXX.

Tonty, Henri de, *Relation of Henri de Tonty Concerning the Explorations of LaSalle from 1678 to 1683* (Chicago: The Caxton Club, 1898) translated by Melville Anderson.

Toupin, Robert, *Les écrits de Pierre Potier: la culture savante en Nouvelle-France au xviii siècle* (Ottawa: Les Presses de L'Université D'Ottawa, 1995).

Trudel, Marcel, *L'Eglise canadienne sous le régime militaire 1759-1764* (Québec: Les Presses Universitaires Laval, 1957).

Washburn and Wilcomb, ed., *The Indian and the White Man* (Garden City, New York: Doubleday and Company, Inc., 1964).

SECONDARY SOURCES

Dionne, M. N.-E., *L'Abbé Gabriel Richard* (Québec: Imprimerie De S.-A. Demers, 1902).

Elliot, Richard R., "Frederick Baraga Among the Ottawas" *The American Catholic Quarterly Review* vol. XXI, No. 81, January, 1896, pp.106-129.

Fagan, Brian, *Clash of Cultures* (New York: W.H. Freeman and Company, 1984).

Ferland, Jean-Baptiste, *La France dans l'Amérique du Nord* (Montréal: Granger Frères Limitée, 1865) vol. III.

Letendre, André, *La Grande aventure des Jésuites au Québec* (Beauport, Québec: Impressions J.L. Inc., 1991).

O'Daniel, V.F., O.P., *The Right Rev. Edward Dominic Fenwick, O.P. Founder of the Dominicans in the United States, Pioneer Missionary in Kentucky, Apostle of Ohio, First Bishop of Cincinnati* (New York: Frederick Pustet Co., 1920).

Paré, George, *The Catholic Church in Detroit 1701-1888* (Detroit: The Gabriel Richard Press, 1951).

Proceedings of the American Antiquarian Society (Worcester, Mass: The Society, 1887).

Rezek, Antoine Ivan, *A History of the Diocese of Sault Ste. Marie and Marquette* (Chicago: M.A. Donohue & Co., 1906) vol. I.

Rochemonteix, Camille de, *Les Jésuites et la Nouvelle-France au xviii siècle* (Paris: Alphonse Picard et Fils Èditeurs, 1906). vol. II.

Stegman, Thomas, "Saint Thomas Aquinas and the Problem of *Akrasia*," *The Modern Schoolman*, LXVI, January 1989, pp. 117-127.

Van Fleet, J.A., *Old and New Mackinac with Copious Extracts from Marquette, Hennepin, La Hontan, Alexander Henry and Others* (Grand Rapids, Mi.: "The Lever" Book and Job Office, 1880).

INDEX